TULSA ART DECO

TULSA ART DECO

AN ARCHITECTURAL ERA 1925-1942

▼

INTRODUCTION BY DAVID GEBHARD

CONTEMPORARY PHOTOGRAPHS BY DAVID HALPERN

THE JUNIOR LEAGUE OF TULSA, INC.
TULSA, OKLAHOMA

FIRST EDITION

Book design by Phillips Knight Walsh, Inc., Tulsa, Oklahoma

Manufactured in the United States of America.

Library of Congress Cataloging in Publication Data

Main entry under title:

Tulsa art deco.

Bibliography: p.
Includes index.
1. Architecture — Oklahoma — Tulsa.
2. Art deco — Oklahoma — Tulsa.
3. Architecture, Modern — 20th century — Oklahoma — Tulsa.
4. Tulsa, Okla. — Buildings.

NA735.T84T84   720'.9766'86   80-21165
ISBN 0-9604368-1-2
ISBN 0-9604368-2-0 (pbk.)

Copies may be ordered from:

Junior League of Tulsa Publications
187 London Square
Tulsa, Oklahoma 74105
918 743-9767

Profits realized from the sale of this book will be returned to the community
through the Junior League of Tulsa's community projects.

A city, in its most real sense, is its buildings.
Whatever the life, spirit, activity,
or achievements of the city may be,
they are expressed in the mass
of asphalt, brick, stone, marble, steel and glass
that has accumulated during the
city's existence.

— Ada Louise Huxtable

FOREWARD

In 1977 the Junior League of Tulsa, Inc. began to study the city's needs in historic preservation. We discovered that Tulsa possessed a wealth of Art Deco buildings which had yet to be documented and which had received only scant attention. Although several of these buildings are architecturally significant by themselves, it is as a group that they reveal much about Tulsa in the 20's and 30's and contribute to our understanding of the Art Deco movement nationally.

We have been extremely fortunate in having two outstanding advisors contribute to this publication. David Gebhard, one of America's foremost experts in Art Deco architecture, agreed to serve as our consultant on the project and to write the book's introduction. A professor of architectural history and the director of the Art Museum at the University of California, Santa Barbara, David organized the first Art Deco exhibition ever held in this country. He has also authored several books on the subject. His contribution to the project has been more than we could have hoped for. He has helped us survey the city, classify and document the Tulsa buildings and has given us a broad look at the development of Art Deco nationally. At his suggestion we included the section on the architectural profession in Tulsa 1925-1940. His enthusiasm for this project and for Tulsa's architectural riches has been contagious.

Since many of the early Zigzag Art Deco structures in Tulsa made elaborate use of terra cotta we needed an expert on the use of this material in the 20's and 30's. Sharon Darling, curator of decorative arts at the Chicago Historical Society, was in the process of producing an exhibit and accompanying book on *Chicago Ceramics & Glass.* Her work is the first research ever done on the terra cotta industry in this country. She was enthusiastic about our project and offered to serve as our terra cotta consultant. Her contribution to the project has been significant and we regret that due to the narrow focus of this book, and to space limitations we were unable to include as much on terra cotta as we would have liked. There is enough interesting material for another book on Tulsa's terra cotta alone.

Our staff consisted of enthusiastic and dedicated volunteers who began their research work as amateur sleuths and quickly became professionals. We logged countless hours in libraries researching city directories, picture files and reading microfilm; in the newspaper morgue; and in the offices of the county clerk and the county assessor researching deeds and property records. We talked to A.I.A. chapters throughout the country as well as to schools, churches, and funeral homes. We even gumshoed around cemetaries looking for some of our missing architects.

In all of our work we were aided by dozens of Tulsans interested in our project and by many who remembered details about Tulsa in the 20's and 30's. Among the young architects practicing in Tulsa in the Deco era, Joseph Koberling, Jr., Frederick Kershner, Donald McCormick and Robert West made invaluable contributions to our research and to our understanding.

Our sleuthing has uncovered the histories of more than fifty-five of Tulsa's Art Deco buildings and biographical information on forty-eight of Tulsa's early architects. We discovered scrapbooks, diaries, photographs and other personal memorabilia. We were elated to discover the Philcade drawings, beautifully detailed in ink on linen; photographs of the Deco murals done by Olinka Hrdy for Riverside Studio; and to find, hidden by a dropped ceiling, the original mezzanine of the Halliburton-Abbott Building with chandelier, carved moldings and etched glass intact.

We have been fortunate in having an able writer on our staff. Carol Johnson has had the awesome task of making the reams of information collected as interesting and alive to the reader as it was to us when we discovered it. We have been proud to have talented local professionals add their creativity to the final product. The photography, the book design and the printing are all done by Tulsans.

Some of us were not sure that we liked Art Deco architecture when we began work on this project but we have all gained an appreciation and an affection for it and our understanding of it has enriched our understanding of the city. We hope that after reading this book no one will ever look at downtown Tulsa in quite the same way. The Art Deco era occurred during Tulsa's boom years and as Tulsa was emerging as a metropolitan area. The character of our city, particularly of its downtown, is still a reflection of that era.

This book is a record of the many Art Deco buildings in Tulsa, those that are still standing and those that have been destroyed. It is also a record of several buildings which were never built or never completed. The rendering of the thirteen-story golden-domed Pythian Building and the drawings of the proposed Art Deco civic center and the streamlined airport terminal tell us a lot about what Tulsa was and what it wanted to be.

In collecting information for this book we were disappointed to find little available on Tulsa architects. We were also disappointed to discover how few of their original drawings had been preserved. Those that are available have been kept by families and business associates. A building is much more than the structure itself and we hope that this publication will stimulate one of our public institutions to collect, store and preserve those records which do exist.

On October 9, 1979 a fifty mile an hour wind blew down the plain wooden facade of LaMaison on 11th Street revealing the original Milady's Cleaners, a terra cotta structure with blue glass windows and elaborate Deco ornamentation in terra cotta and cast iron. The owners called it "an act of God" and began careful work on its restoration so that it could be photographed for our book. We hope that this book will be the catalyst for the discovery of many other Art Deco treasures presently concealed by years of neglect.

Finally we hope that in having documented Tulsa's Art Deco architecture, we may interest other cities, particularly in the Southwest, to reflect upon their own architectural heritage.

Susan Petersmeyer Henneke
Editor

ACKNOWLEDGMENTS

The contributions of many people are reflected in this book but our first words of warm appreciation must go to Joseph R. Koberling, Jr., Donald McCormick, Robert West, Bruce Goff, William Wolaver and the late Frederick Vance Kershner. These six architects acted as our guides to the era of Art Deco Architecture in Tulsa. Their work is represented in this volume, but we are also indebted to them for providing us with anecdotes, names, dates, and memories of their early years in practice.

Mary Collins, Chairman of the Junior League Historic Preservation Project 1979-1980, was an enthusiastic advocate and assumed responsibility for many of the details involved in this book's production. Members of the project Advisory Board were helpful individually and collectively in directing the project and in contributing to our research. Our thanks to David Breed, Roger Cole Coffey, Joe Coleman, Tamara Coombs, Evans Dunn, Greta Faith, Fred Falls, Dr. Nancy Feldman, Beryl Ford, Russell Gideon, Tom Goodgame, Robert B. Hardy, Mayor James M. Inhofe, David Jones, Dr. Guy Logsdon, Harley Manhart, Minnie Kennedy Manion, J. Barlow Nelson, and Dr. William A. Settle, Jr.

Dan P. Holmes, Maurice Devinna, Mrs. A. L. Farmer, Walton Clinton, Mrs. Wilbur J. Holliman, Mr. and Mrs. Martin Wiesendanger, Mrs. Buford Monnet, William Gay and Clarence Allen shared with us their rich knowledge of Tulsa in the 20's and 30's.

Many of the architects currently practicing in Tulsa were helpful, especially: H. G. Barnard, David E. Broach, Garth W. Caylor, Jr., Roger C. Coffey, Mary Caroline Cole, Joe Coleman, John Cushing, Robert L. Jones, Gordon McCune, Dennis Manasco, Paul L. Murphy, David G. Murray, Thomas Thixton, and Wallace O. Wozencraft.

Earl Bragdon was an invaluable resource for his knowledge of the building industry in Tulsa in the 20's and 30's and of the structural glass business. Several people made substantial contributions to specific areas of our research: Jack Whitacre, ornamental glass; Mrs. W. J. Smiley and Ernest Wieman, lighting fixtures and metal work; H. P. Primm and Ray Luttrell, neon; Sharon S. Darling, Trygve Kristiansen, Alice J. Reen, George A. Berry, and K. C. Burns, terra cotta and the terra cotta industry; Mrs. G. W. Cottrell, Edwin Pernier, Hugh J. Wirsching and Richard McMahon, marble and tile.

Many people contributed specific information on buildings, their architects and clients and went out of their way to help us. We are grateful to Mrs. Cecil Albert, Robert Allen, Larkin Bailey, Ben Ball, Mrs. John Bartram, Mr. and Mrs. Ralph Bendel, Mrs. Charles W. Bliss, John Bliss, Reverend Donald W. Brooks, Mrs. Vincent Carothers, David Delong, William Doty, J. D. Duncan, John Elsner, Charles B. Grant, Mr. and Mrs. Ray D. Grimshaw, Jr., Robert B. Hardy, Dr. William T. Holland, Richard Huckett, Lorraine Huntze, Ray Jordan, Glade Kirpatrick, Alvin Krumrey, T. N. Law, Jim Lieberman, Henry R. Lohman, Mrs. J. W. McCollum, Mary McGovern, Richard Martinez, Charles C. Mason, Mrs. John Mattern, Mr. and Mrs. Allen Mayo, Burch Mayo, Dr. Joseph Millichap, Lee Mulhall, Scottie Page, Sid Patterson, Ike Parkey, Dr. Rick Pickard, Hazel Pierce, Larry Rooney, Isadore Shank, Jack Schupert, W. A. Setser, Mrs. H. J. Sherman, Charles Smith, Jon R. Stuart, Jere Uncapher, Mrs. Arnold Ungerman, Martha Trindle, Clyde Walker, William Waller, Ed Wheeler, Mrs. Phillip H. Wilber, Reverend James D. White, Mrs. A. S. Whitlock, and Douglas Wixon.

The biographical sketches of the architects practicing in Tulsa, 1925-1940, would not have been possible without the help of their friends and relatives. Our thanks to Mrs. Carl Abshire, Ross B. Baze, Mrs. Ralph Black, Sr., Ralph M. Black, Jr., Mrs. John T. Blair, Clarence H. Blue, Harry B. Blue, Gustav Brandborg, Mrs. Leslie Brooks, Mrs. Willaim Calderwood, Nancy Calderwood, Virginia B. Clary, Marshall Cross, Jr., Mrs. Frederick Duggan, Jack A. Endacott, Mark Endacott, Richard Endacott, Mrs. Edith Deal Ache Forsyth, Justine Gillian, Mary Ann Hamm, Mrs. C. C. Knoblock, Theodore Kubatzky, Mrs. A. Garland Marrs, Mrs. Donald McCormick, Mrs. Malcolm L. McCune, John T. Murphy, Beverly Nelson, Jr., Mrs. Frank M. Olston, Sequoah Perry, Mrs. P. W. Perryman, Mrs. Harley T. Price, Mr. H. Pruitt, John Reid, Edward F. Saunders, Jr., J. F. Shumway, Dr. Mary Edna Sippel, Mrs. Edward L. Wilson, Geroge A. Winkler, Jr., and Mrs. H. M. Winter.

Many staff members of various organizations we contacted were particularly helpful. Among these were: Alice Morgan, Maureen Marx, and Deepa Mahhavan, American Institute of Architects, Washington, D. C.; Mabel Krank, American Institute of Architects, Oklahoma City; Marilyn Hooper, American Institute of Architects, Tulsa; Richard Drew, American Petroleum Institute, Washington, D. C.; Lexie Hopkins, Board of Governors of Licensed Architects, Oklahoma City; Mrs. George Metzel, Boston Avenue Methodist Church Archives, Tulsa; Frank Jewell, Chicago Historical Society; Morgan Powell, Education Service Center, Tulsa; Bruce Pieffer, Frank Lloyd Wright Foundation, Scottsdale, Arizona; Gordon Olsen, Kent County Library, Grand Rapids, Michigan; Cataloging and Reference Librarians, McFarlin Library, University of Tulsa; Diane Maddex, National Trust for Historic Preservation, Washington, D. C.; Tamara Coombs, National Trust for Historic Preservation, Oklahoma City; Dr. Alan Brunken, Dr. John Bryant and Dr. George Chamberlaine, School of Architecture, Oklahoma State University; Jesse Wright, Marcia Manhart and Tom Young, Philbrook Art Center, Tulsa; Sharon Meeks, Will Rogers High School, Tulsa; Clyde Cole, John Barhydt and Bruce Carnet, Tulsa Chamber of Commerce; Reference Librarians, Tulsa City County Library; Elta Baldridge, Tulsa Club; Office of Tulsa County Assessor; Office of Tulsa County Clerk; Suzanne Boles, Tulsa County Historical Society; Fred Falls and Michael Stewart, Tulsa Historic Preservation Office; Imogene Arnot, Tulsa Municipal Airport Authority; Staff of *Tulsa World/ Tulsa Tribune* Library; Dr. Leonard Eaton, School of Architecture, University of Michigan; Alan K. Lathrop, Northwest Architectural Archives, University of Minnesota; Louise Choate, Webster High School, Tulsa.

Tulsans who graciously allowed us to photograph their homes include: Mr. and Mrs. J. D. Bass, Mr. and Mrs. Gary M. Cook, Mr. and Mrs. Jesse D. Davis, Mr. and Mrs. J. B. McGay, Mr. and Mrs. Peter J. McMahon, Mr. and Mrs. James D. Mayfield, Dr. and Mrs. Henry H. Modrak, Dr. and Mrs. Franklin Nelson, Mr. and Mrs. Gary Phillips, and Mrs. Leslie J. Seidenbach.

The photographic talent of David Halpern assisted by Lynn Endres is evident throughout the book but we are also especially indebted to those who made their old photographs, renderings and architectural drawings available to us: Mrs. Howard G. Barnett, Beryl Ford, Bruce Goff, Howard Hopkins, Olinka Hrdy, Dennis Manasco, Bob McCormack, Donald McCormick,

Mrs. Murray McCune, Joseph McNulty, Martin M. Pomphrey, John Steiger, and Mrs. Jack Talbot.

We would like to express our thanks to Susan Dunn, Sylvia McCormick Campbell and Laura Martens for their help in the research; Karen Fraser for her help with a multitude of details; Francine Ringold and Maureen Modlish for their editorial assistance; Ann Patterson and Carole Raulston for typing the manuscript; Linda Lambert and Linda Frazier, presidents of the Junior League of Tulsa, Inc. 1979-1980 and 1980-1981, for their support and encouragement.

Special thanks must go to our families who endured endless meetings, telephone calls, missed meals and weekends of work and who remained supportive and patient. We are grateful to them for making our efforts on this publication possible.

Lastly, we are indebted to David Gebhard for sharing his extensive knowledge of Art Deco architecture with us. For all that he taught us to see and to appreciate and, most of all, for his genuine enthusiasm for this project and his unwavering confidence in us, we thank him.

Editor —
Susan Petersmeyer Henneke

Author —
Carol Newton Johnson

Researchers —
Melissa Potter Atkinson
Claudia Kates Doyle
Frances Frawley Swanson
Francesanne McFadyen Tucker
Sybil Beard Tyler

Art Director —
Carol McLemore Pielsticker

INTRODUCTION

David Gebhard

One of the central delights of history — and particularly the history of the recent past — is the way in which we reject an episode at one moment and embrace it in the next. During the decades of the 1940's through the 1960's no aspect of architecture was held more in disdain than that of the Art Deco of the twenties and thirties. Art Deco, the popularized modern of these decades, was either ignored by our major architects and writers, or it was dismissed as an unfortunate, obviously misguided effort; the sooner it was forgotten the better. Those who exposed high art modernism during the thirty years from 1940 to 1970 condemned the Art Deco for preserving too many traditional architectural values, for being too concerned with the decorative arts and popular symbolism, and for being too compromising in its acceptance of the imagery of high art modern architecture of the twenties and thirties.

All of these accusations against the Art Deco were true — the difference today is that we are inclined to feel that all of these qualities which were looked upon so disdainfully were, in fact, assets, not defects. Having now experienced thirty years of modern architecture we are not at all sure that this is in truth the world in which we wish to live. The richness, the variety of Art Deco modes of the near-past offer us a decided relief from the boring dullness of so much of the modern architecture of recent years.

Our current involvement with the Art Deco is also closely tied to our concerns for historic preservation. The downtowns of America's cities contain (or did contain) numerous Art Deco skyscrapers of the late 1920's and early 1930's, and the commitment to the automobile at the end of the thirties resulted in the splendid development of Streamline Art Deco roadside strip architecture. Both the earlier Art Deco skyscrapers and the later Streamline Art Deco roadside buildings have suffered from ruthless destruction or insensitive alterations over the past three decades. It is now apparent that there will not be much left of this significant phase of America's architectural inheritance unless a conscious effort is made to preserve it.

It has been pointed out that on the surface the closest bedfellow to Art Deco is Art Nouveau, another relatively recent movement which was heartily despised by architects and scholars even during its heyday and immediately after. Since the late 1940's it has been given a newly recognized place in architecture and art history. There is, though, an important difference between the Art Nouveau and the Art Deco, for the former was in every sense of the term a refined high art elitist style, while the latter was popular and middle-class. One suspects that much of the later modernist rejection of the Art Deco had to do not with the style itself, but with its popular acceptance. It was too middle-class and it was not elitist enough to satisfy the more "high-falutin'" pretense of intellectuals and architects of the post World War II years.

The history of art and of architecture are saddled with style terms—Gothic, Baroque, Rococo, etc., all of which became popular coinage for anything but logical reasons. The same holds true for the name Art Deco. This term was coined at the end of the 1960's by the English historian Bevis Hillier. The term Art Deco was not at all common during the twenties and thirties—but that doesn't matter, it is generally accepted today, so we will use it. There are several built-in difficulties with the use of the term Art Deco; the term is used to describe three separate but related movements of the popular modern architecture which took place during these years. The first style was in part derived from the famous 1925 Exposition of the Decorative Arts in Paris. This style, which has been labeled the Zigzag Art Deco, was the essential ingredient of what came to be referred to at the time as the American Perpendicular Skyscraper Style. The second of the Art Deco styles was a symbolism of industry and the machine based on the aerodynamic imagery of streamlining; it appears in industrial designs as the aerodynamic teardrop form; in architecture it manifests itself through white stucco or concrete walls, curved facades and glass bricks. The third of the Art Deco styles was an International Stripped Classicism which we in America closely associated with the Great Depression, the New Deal, the PWA and Franklin Delano Roosevelt; in Europe at the time we associated it with the "Fascist" architecture of Hitler and Mussolini. This abstracted, puritanical classicism was of course far more international than the much-touted Modern International style. If we can see that the Art Deco was in reality three related but distinct styles, then we can better understand it. Each of these phases of Art Deco—the Zigzag Art Deco of the twenties, the Streamline Art Deco of the thirties, and the PWA Classical-oriented Art Deco of the thirties—developed its own highly individual architectural vocabularies to preach the now (the Modern), but at the same time retained a strong link with tradition and the past.

The romantic view of the downtown of the American city as a forest of skyscraper towers separated by deep misty canyons of streets, was a product of a surprisingly brief moment in history. The landscape of towers and chasms, so vividly depicted in the drawings of the 1920's and early 30's of Hugh Ferriss, came into being during the seven years of frenzied building activities between 1925 and 1931. The reaction of Americans at the time to this symbolic and factual form of the new city was, as always, complex and contradictory. The vertical forest of towers rising in the landscape evoked an image closely linked to the nineteenth century view of the Gothic past as a golden age. But at the same time the image of the skyscraper was closely tied in the popular mind to the preeminence of American businesses of the day, and to the glories of a practical technological future which, it seemed then, unquestionably lay in store for America.

For Americans of the teens and twenties the ideal realization of the new city was New York's Manhattan Island. To one degree or another every American city worth its salt tried to emulate the visual experience of New York, and that experience was summed up in a single building type—the office skyscraper. Both factually and symbolically the skyscraper embraced American ideals during the late twenties and opening years of the thirties. The sheer number built, their ever increasing height, forcefully conveyed America's commitment to rapid change and progress. The skyscraper asserted the essential qualities of laissez-faire business, ranging from the virtues of intensified land use, to the developing complexities of business bureaucracy and the successful expression of practical American technology.

While the task of America in the twenties was business, its reason for being was the home—and generally speaking the two existed in separate, hermetically sealed compartments. From the nineteenth century to the present the ideal of a detached house in the suburbs or country remained as the most constant of American ideals. Through the early years of the 1920's the suburban ideal was almost exclusively tied to the suburban train or street railway. It was *the* machine of the twenties—the automobile—which changed all of this. Suburbia on the scale needed was now possible not only for America's upper middle class, but for the expanding middle class as well. The automobile not only made suburbia possible, but it introduced a variety of new land uses and building types. The street or highway connecting downtown with suburbia blossomed forth with an array of auto-oriented buildings, ranging from gas stations to drive-in restaurants. Normal day to day retail shopping began to cluster along the roadside and eventually began to congeal into small and large neighborhood shopping centers. Increasingly the downtown shopping experience became a more specialized experience, separated from the satisfaction of daily needs now fulfilled at the suburban supermarket, drugstore or dry cleaner.

The late twenties and early thirties employed a rich palate of architectural images to package this complex and more often than not contradicting urban/suburban scene. At the beginning of the twenties the fashionable garb for the skyscraper was Classical or Gothic with a predominance of the former. By the mid-twenties, with the well publicized success of Howell and Hood's Tribune Tower in Chicago (1922-24), the Gothic had asserted its preeminence. At the end of the decade both the Gothic and the Classical experienced a transformation toward the Modern. Goodhue's tower for the Nebraska State Capital at Lincoln (1916-28) aptly demonstrated that the Classical tradition could, through a process of simplification, be responded to as both traditional and modern. Likewise the Gothic could be stripped down to its vertical essentials, as Eliel Saarinen did in his highly publicized second prize design for the Chicago Tribune Tower (1922), or in Howell and Hood's somewhat later American Radiator Building in New York (1924), and then it too, could emerge as an image which offered the comfort of the past coupled with a look into the future.

The continual modernization of traditional imagery which occurred during this decade paved the way for one of the new fashionable styles of this century, that of the Art Deco (the Moderne). As a style the Art Deco provided a gentle transition to the new age without in any way severing our ties with the past. The abstracted Classic and Gothic skyscrapers of the late twenties had suggested that we could have the best of both the past and the future; the Art Deco went one step further and said it is here now! It accomplished the "here it is" primarily by employing the full range of decorative art that had come to be seen by its middle class audience as "modernistic." It was the decorative elements, more than any other single feature, which urged us to respond to a building as Art Deco as opposed to it being Traditional. The Art Deco Zigzag vocabulary of chevrons, triangles, stepped patterns, spirals, fronds, etc., often realized through brilliant "pure" colors, were the architectural elements which then and now prompt us to label a building as Art Deco. In most instances, if we were to replace the decorative detailing of a Art Deco skyscraper with a Classical, Romanesque or Gothic ornament, we would then respond to it as Byzantine, Gothic or Classical.

The one and occasional two and three-story commercial buildings which occurred on the outskirts of a city's downtown core, or along the developing commercial strips, and in the new suburban shopping centers tended to vary their imagery over a broader spectrum during the late 1920's and early 1930's. A few of these smaller commercial buildings, garages, car agencies, service stations and markets situated on the outskirts of downtown were clothed in the latest Art Deco. But most of the low-rise commercial buildings which surrounded the downtown core were meant to be experienced as down-to-earth practical utilitarian structures. They were modern (with a small "m") because they were meant to be a functional response to need. If "art" entered into their design it was dealt with in a reserved parsimonious fashion.

Proceeding from the high-rise core of downtown to its periphery of low one, two and three-story commercial buildings, one discovers a real potpourri of architectural imagery, ranging from the Classical, Gothic and Art Deco, to straightforward utilitarian structures. Generally, the most apparent element in these buildings was their signing—for the signs not only let us know what was going on in the buildings, they were the principal feature which established the character of the establishment. At night these signs, coupled with the usual array of outdoor billboards, asserted their indisputable primacy; the buildings tend to disappear in the dark mist of the night.

A few of these buildings sought to put on some architectural pretense. This was especially true of such businesses as mortuaries, dry-cleaning establishments, cat and dog hospitals and printing plants. By the end of the twenties the Art Deco had emerged as a favored image for these and other smaller-scaled buildings. Most of them were sheathed in traditional brick with just the right amount of decorative terra cotta ornament. Their plans and elevations were almost always symmetrical. The walls were vertically articulated by projecting piers which often extended above the parapet of the building.

The smaller, more auto-oriented commercial buildings, which occured along the major thoroughfares as they extended out to suburbia, tended to be much more mixed in their imagery. The earlier gasoline service stations were generally direct and utilitarian, but very soon they assumed one or another of the then current architectural poses. As one approached and entered suburbia itself, the characteristic service station and other types of commercial buildings attired themselves in domestic garb — the Colonial Revival and Tudor in the East and Midwest, and the Spanish Colonial Revival and other exotic variations in the Southwest and in California. It would be natural to assume that the Art Deco would have been a favored image for suburban service stations; but that was not the case until after 1930. Of the limited number which were built in this style, most were situated, not in suburbia or along the thoroughfares leading to suburbia, but along the entrances/exits of the principal intercity highways.

In suburbia itself, traditional imagery remained supreme. With the exception of California and Florida, with their regional preferences for the Mediterranean and Spanish Colonial Revival, the rest of suburban America had a decided preference for the English Tudor, the French Norman and the American Colonial. The concept of domesticity, of the family and of home, could not very easily be accommodated in a house planned and conceived of as an Art Deco object. While there were a certain number of Art Deco apartment houses built throughout the country, there were only a small number of residences built in the style. If we look into the biography of each of these Art Deco houses of the twenties we will almost always discover a special commitment on the part of the client to modernistic art.

So far no mention has been made of residential and non-residential architecture of the years 1920-1930 which we would call Modern (International Style) with a capital "M." The truth is that there were very few High Art Modern buildings constructed in the United States prior to 1930. The principal group of these occurred in and around Los Angeles and were the work of either R. M. Schindler or Richard J. Neutra. The Midwest was devoid of any Modern buildings at the time, and in the Northeast there was a small sprinkling of Modern structures designed by Oscar Stonorov, Howe and Lescaze, Kocher and Frey and a few others.

Finally, there was a small contingent of designers which were indeed Modern, but who do not fit comfortably into any of the then-current styles. Foremost among these were Frank Lloyd Wright, his oldest son Lloyd Wright, Barry Byrne and Bruce Goff. While the work of all these designers was thought of as avant-garde at the time, their highly individualistic designs closely reflected a number of the major trends of the time, including the Art Deco, the exotic, non-European historicism, plus a healthy dose of European Expressionism.

As a professional, the American architect had arrived by the twenties. The profession, through the continued intervention of the A.I.A., had established licensing in the states — the architect was now to be treated as the other professionals in medicine and law. Education in architecture became common at most public and private universities, and the studio approach of the French Ecole Beaux Arts became the norm. The opulent twenties provided a glut of commissions for a good number of America's architectural firms. Large scaled firms developed in every major city. The axiom "America's task was business" was mirrored in the organization and approach to the production of buildings by these major firms. By the end of the decade the ability of the profession to produce functional, well-detailed and constructed buildings was close to perfection. In the area of design there was a steady tendency for these buildings to become increasingly competent. The Beaux Arts insistence on logical order, balance and proportions made it difficult for any building's design to go wrong—whether Gothic, Classical, or Art Deco.

Mention has already been made of the abstracting process through which the Classical tradition went in the 1920's. In the work of the three pre-eminent exponents of this process, Bertram G. Goodhue, Harold Van Buren Magonigle and Paul Cret, the adherence to classical principles of plan, massing and detailing remained unaltered. But slowly, at the end of the twenties, Art Deco elements began to creep into the Classical tradition. By 1930 a distinct recognizable version of the Classical tradition had come into being. Government buildings, ranging from Federal Court Houses and Post Offices to county and city buildings, adopted this image, as did financial institutions which always like to pretend that they are somehow governmental. Though this mode was fully established by 1932 when Franklin D. Roosevelt became president, it came to be quickly associated with the New Deal and its extensive building program. Today we label the style of these Classical-oriented buildings as PWA Art Deco (Modernes) because so many were a product of PWA Federal funding. But we must not lose sight of the fact that this classical abstracting process went back to the early 1920's (and even before), and that it was a world-wide phenomenon which was equally reflected, as we have already noted, in the architecture of Fascist Italy and Nazi Germany.

Commercial buildings which exhibit the Zigzag phase of the Art Deco continued to be built on into the late 1930's, but by that time they were old-fashioned. The new popular version of the Art Deco during the Depression years was the Streamline. The image of the curve, of the aerodynamic teardrop, suggestive of speed, became the predominant symbol of the present and of the future. The traditional sense of mass was replaced by thin volumed stucco boxes whose ornament consisted of curved surfaces, walls of horizontal glass bricks, and occasional surfaces sheathed in Vitrolite or baked enamel panels. The design elements of the Streamline Art Deco were limited in number, which among other things meant that the application of just a few elements was all that was necessary to create the image of the new age.

In the downtown areas of the American city the economic effects of the Great Depression meant that few large-scaled commercial buildings were built. There was a marked tendency to remodel store and restaurant fronts—something which could be inexpensively accomplished by the injection of a few curved surfaces and windows, glass brick, Vitrolite panels and neon lights. The application of these materials could instantly transform an old-fashioned bar, drugstore or restaurant into the latest fashion. On the outskirts of the downtown similar transformations took place, accompanied at the end of the thirties by new Streamline Art Deco buildings to house auto salesrooms and other establishments.

Commercial strips leading to suburbia, and alongside the principal intercity highways experienced a major building boom between 1937 and 1942, and the Steamline Art Deco was the predominant architectural style. Service stations, drive-in fast food places, suburban moviehouses, laundries, supermarkets and the rest of the highway commercial buildings were close to universal in their employment of the style. While there were still neighborhood shopping centers, occasional restaurants and service stations which continued to clothe themselves in Colonial or Spanish Colonial Revival imagery, the Streamline Art Deco came close to providing an American Style which united all strip commercial, regional and neighborhood shopping centers.

As in the previous decade the Streamline Art Deco was not a favored domestic image, but still it is surprising how many Streamline residences were built in the suburban areas of the U.S. Once again it was the client, who more often than not, pressed for an avant-garde image. Generally, the clients of these Moderne houses were individuals involved with construction, the oil and gas industry, or were physicians or veterinarians. A look into the history of many of these houses shows that it was the woman who was the most involved in the specifics of the design process, but the sense of conveying the most scientific and up-to-date (and the image of the Machine) must have reflected the joint feeling of both wife and husband. In plan, Streamline Art Deco houses were essentially the same as one would find in contemporary Colonial or Monterey Colonial houses. But the flat parapeted roofs, white stucco walls, curved corner windows, metal sash windows and glass brick pressed us then and now to respond to them as Art Deco.

While there were an increased number of high art Modern (International Style) houses and other buildings constructed in the thirties, the number was small. The two centers for the doctrinaire Modern were still Southern California and the Northeast. In the Midwest, George Fred Keck and a few other designers introduced the stringent principle of the style, but the dividing line between the Modern and the Streamline Art Deco is often so obscure that it is difficult to know whether we should call it one or the other. In a way it may well be meaningless for us to make such precise distinctions, for all of these buildings and houses were meant to be responded to as modern by those living at the time. The extremes at each end are easy to recognize — a Modern Los Angeles house (like the Beard house, 1935, by Richard J. Neutra); or a Streamline Art Deco Texaco service station (1936) by Walter Dorwin Teague; but everything between tends to mix their imagery.

Like the rest of the U.S. in the twenties, the Midwest, extending from Minneapolis/St. Paul to the eastern reaches of the Southwest, Oklahoma City and Tulsa, experienced a tremendous building boom. This boom was almost exclusively confined to the large urban environments; smaller cities and towns remained relatively stationary, reflecting in part the poor economic conditions of farming during this decade. With the ease of communications and the universality of the Beaux Arts architectural education systems, it should not be surprising that there was little or no time-lag between when a new fashion was adopted in New York or Chicago, and when it occurred in the principal Midwestern and Southwestern cities. To be sure there were certain prestigious architectural firms which established that which was the latest — Howell and Hood in New York, or Holabird and Root in Chicago — but their imagery was taken up as quickly in Kansas City or Tulsa, as it was by other architects in New York or Chicago. A similar nationwide contemporaneousness occurred with the Streamline Art Deco. While the principal proponents of the Streamline, the industrial designers Raymond Loewy, Walter Dorwin Teague, Norman Bel Geddes and Howard Van Doren were New York based, the streamlining of buildings in the Midwest occurred at the same moment as it occurred on Manhatten Island.

In looking into the history of the popular Art Deco — its early Zigzag phase, its later Streamline phase, and its PWA offshoot — it is intriguing to note that the American Midwest ended up housing a number of its principal monuments. These range from Bertram G. Goodhue's Nebraska State Capital Building in Lincoln (1916-1928), to Harold Van Buren Magonigle's Liberty Memorial in Kansas City (1923-1926), to Holabird and Root's (with Ellerbe Architects) St. Paul City Hall and Ramsey County Court House in St. Paul (1931-32), to the crowning jewel of the Streamline Art Deco, Frank Lloyd Wright's administrative offices for the Johnson Wax Company in Racine, Wisconsin (1936-1939). The occurrence of these and other monuments to the Art Deco in the Midwest and the Southwest do not in any way indicate that this region was preeminent in this mode; rather, it illustrates how closely architects, clients and their public audience responded to the rapidly changing taste on a national level.

A classic example of how comfortably the Midwest and the Southwest fitted into the national scene during the twenties and thirties can be seen by turning our attention to a single city — that of Tulsa, Oklahoma. This urban environment provides an excellent case study of changes in architectural imagery, for it was within these two decades that Tulsa emerged as a major metropolitan area. With its economy based upon the oil and gas industry, it was in every sense a product of its age — and as such, it self-consciously sought to reflect this in its urban and suburban architecture.

By 1930 Tulsa had acquired the needed image of a modern twentieth century city — a group of moderate to tall skyscrapers to define its downtown, and then the usually horizontal spread of low-rise commercial buildings which trailed out to upper middle class suburbia. As with a number of other cities in the Midwest and the Southwest Tulsa's skyscrapers seem to rise directly from the undulating prairies, providing the ultimate in asserting the presence of a real city. Tulsa went through the usual set of images for the skyscraper before it settled down to the Zigzag Art Deco at the end of the twenties. The city's first skyscraper was the sixteen-story Cosden Building (1916), which was clothed in classical garb; at the end of the twenties this was joined by the Philtower (Delk; Keene and Simpson 1927-1928) which though Gothic in spirit, entailed elements inspired by the stripped classicism of Bertram G. Goodhue, and the crisp decorative surfaces and ornament which we associate with the Art Deco. A similar mixing took place in the Beaux Arts-styled National Bank of Tulsa (Weary and Alford, 1918 and 1922) where later the twenty-seven story central tower appreciably reflected the Art Deco.

In Tulsa, Zigzag Art Deco skyscrapers arrived on the scene during the years 1927-1928. The Medical and Dental Arts Building of 1927 (Arthur M. Atkinson; Joseph R. Koberling, Jr.) conveyed a slight Gothic flavor in many of its details and above all in its strong emphasis on verticality. Like many other Zigzag Art Deco skyscrapers in Tulsa and elsewhere, the Medical and Dental Arts Building employed terra cotta extensively, both on its exterior and in its interior. The Medical and Dental Arts Building was followed by a succession of mild to strong Art Deco commercial blocks and skyscrapers — the ten-story Oklahoma Natural Gas Building (Arthur M. Atkinson; Frederick V. Kershner, 1928); the five-story Public Service Building (Arthur M. Atkinson; Joseph R. Koberling, 1929); the ten-story Bliss Hotel (Leland I. Shumway, 1929); and the seven-story Halliburton-Abbott Building Department Store (Frank C. Walter, 1929). Reflecting the general optimisim of the time, both the Halliburton-Abbott Building and the Public Service Building were designed so that additional floors could be added. All of these buildings display the patterns and motifs we associate with the early Art Deco — zigzags, chevrons, spirals, fronds, half-circles and the like. These designs were realized in glazed and unglazed terra cotta, cast plaster, tile, metal, glass, stencils and paint.

What would have been the crowning glory of the early Art Deco in Tulsa was the Gillette-Tyrrell (Pythian) Building (Edward W. Saunders, 1930). Only the first three floors of what was to have been a thirteen-story skyscraper were realized before the advent of the Depression. The striking emphasis on verticality conveyed by the linear pattern of terra cotta gives an almost Expressionist quality to the building's exterior, and the L-shaped two-story lobby, with its multicolored walls and floors of multicolored tile — browns, blues, reds, greens — suggest a variety of exotic influences ranging from the pre-Columbian to the Islamic and Egyptian.

While one must speak of what could have been in the case of the Gillette-Tyrrell (Pythian) Building, the interior L-shaped public corridor of the 1930 Philcade (Smith and Senter) constitutes one of the great Zigazg Art Deco interior spaces in America. The sense conveyed is that of richness of surfaces and details, most of which are of a metallic finish which was adroitly emphasized by interior lighting. The general feel of luxury that this interior detailing performs is the perfect task of the Art Deco — to have one foot in the past and one in the present and near-future.

As with other American cities a number of small-scaled Art Deco buildings were constructed on the periphery of Tulsa's downtown and further out. Of these the Warehouse Market (B. Gaylord Noftsger, 1929) with its brilliant red, blue and white glazed terra cotta is an especially fine example of the style. And fitting, for the "Oil Capital of The World," was the Mid-Continent Oil Company (Diamond DX) service station at nearby Sapulpa, Oklahoma designed by the Tulsa architect, Donald McCormick in 1931. This station was sheathed in polished black glass (including the gasoline pumps themselves), which theatrically contrasted with the cream and red glass in diamond patterns, and red lettering.

As already indicated, the PWA Art Deco provided a logical transition between the Zigzag Art Deco of the twenties and the Streamline Art Deco of the next decade. Buildings devoted to transportation beautifully mirror the changes in PWA Art Deco in Tulsa. The 1931 Union Depot (R. C. Stephens) is heftily monumental with references to the pre-Art Deco world of Otto Wagner in Vienna, Eliel Saarinen in Finland, and Bertram G. Goodhue in the U.S. The next two transportation buildings, that for buses and that for the airplane, pulls us partially over into the Streamline Art Deco of the 1930's. The original proposal for the Tulsa Municipal Airport Terminal and Administration Building was as way-out in its streamlining as one could ask (designed by Jesse L. Bowling and Isadore Shank). The spirit of this Buck Rogers streamlining takes us directly back to Eric Mendelsohn's theoretical drawings of the teens and his 1919 Einstein Tower at Potsdam. The Airport Terminal Building, which was constructed between 1931 and 1932 (Smith and Senter; F. V. Kershner) was certainly a more conservative and correct version of the PWA Art Deco, with its delicate balance between the earlier design principles of the Beaux Arts and the new lightness of the streamline with emphasis on the horizontal, rounded corners and extensive transparent glass. The final transportation building which embraced the PWA Art Deco was the Union Bus Depot (Smith and Senter; F. V. Kershner, 1934-1935). Originally, the Bus Depot was to have been combined with an adjacent seven-story hotel (designed by Smith and Senter, 1934), but this more ambitious scheme was abandoned, and just the Depot was built. When completed it was described as being "modernistic" in the local press. The culmination of the composition was the tall (40 foot plus) free standing neon sign which stood at the corner of the property. The building itself, with its horizontal banded surface of cream colored stucco, red brick and terra cotta, served as a backdrop to the dramatic sign, and the hustle and bustle of the buses in front of the building.

There were other public Tulsa buildings which carried on the design principle of the PWA Art Deco. These include the Tulsa Fire Alarm Building (Smith and Senter; F. V. Kershner, 1931) with its sumptuous sculptured program in terra cotta, and the Pavilion of the Tulsa State Fairgrounds (L. I. Shumway, 1932), with its terra cotta ornamentation depicting horses, steers, rams and stylized plants. Toward the end of the thirties two extensive educational plants were built in Tulsa which exemplify the design predilection of the PWA Art Deco. These were Webster High School (John D. Forsyth, William H. Wolaver, Raymond Kerr and A. M. Atkinson, 1938), and Will Rogers High School (Leon B. Senter; Joseph R. Koberling, Jr.; A. M. Atkinson, 1938): both of these schools are campus schemes laid out on extensive sites. Of the two, the Will Rogers High School building employed more ornament and adhered more strongly to the classical design principles of the earlier PWA Art Deco. The Webster High School building with its suggestion of the Streamline indicates that its designers were more abreast of what was the latest fashion.

The three architects who brought almost instant recognition to Tulsa during these decades were Barry Byrne, Bruce Goff and Frank Lloyd Wright. Byrne's Expressionistic Christ the King Church (1926) was an influential design, not only affecting the work in Tulsa of Bruce Goff, but having an impact in other areas of the country. Detroit's Shrine of the Little Flower of 1929-1933 (Henry McGill), and Lloyd Wright's project of 1931 for the Roman Catholic Cathedral in Los Angeles, indicate that Byrne's exercise in Expressionism was influential in the approach which the Roman Catholic Church began to take toward modern architecture.

Bruce Goff's work in Tulsa, first as a draftsman/designer for Rush, Endacott and Rush, and later as a partner in Endacott and Goff, indicates how well an architect could keep well abreast of changing fashions, without actually knowing most of the work firsthand. All of Goff's designs ca. 1930 display his own, at times mad version of architectural Expressionism. Such buildings as his Guaranty Laundry (1928), the Midwest Equitable Meter

Company (1929), the Page Warehouse (1927), the Tulsa Club (1927), the Riverside Studio (1929) and the Merchants Exhibit Building of the Tulsa State Fairgrounds (1930) are little known, but major works within twentieth-century American architecture. The one design of Goff, which was well publicized at the time, was the Boston Avenue Methodist Church (1929) which, in its imagery comes the closest of any of his works to mirroring the fashion of the Zigzag Art Deco and of his highly personal version of Expressionism. A twilight view of the thrusting tower of this church could easily be mistaken for an actualization of one of the drawings of Hugh Ferriss.

The architect which Goff most admired, Frank Lloyd Wright, was also strongly affected by the twenties Zigzag Art Deco as well as European Expressionism. When finished in 1929, his Lloyd Jones house in suburban Tulsa could easily pass for a scale-less factory on the Prairie. Its rhythm of narrow vertical piers might just as well be the walls of a many-storied industrial building rather than those of an upper middle class suburban home.

Tulsa's Streamline Art Deco entail all of the building types which we associate with this late version of the popular Moderne. Service stations (especially a good number of Walter Dorwin Teague's 1936 Texaco stations), veterinary clinics, small banks and the like sported the style. Three of the city's theaters were of streamline design; and one, the Will Rogers Theater (Jack Corgan and W. J. Moore, 1941) with its marquee wrapped around its pencil-like tower, is an outstanding example of the style. Important also for the history of the Streamline Art Deco and of drive-in architecture were the chain of Silver Castles which were started in Tulsa in 1936. By 1941 there were nine of these fast food, auto-oriented restaurants in operation in Tulsa and, as their designs evolved, they became increasingly streamline.

The city's most unique contribution to the Streamline Art Deco is to be found in the suburban upper middle class residences built in this mode. While most large and small U.S. urban centers contain a sprinkling of residences in this Art Deco style, few can equal the quantity and quality found in Tulsa. Between the years 1935 and 1940 nine of these residences were built, and several of them, such as the Forsyth Residence (John D. Forsyth; Robert E. West, 1937), the Fleeger Residence (Frederick V. Kershner, 1937), the Shakley Residence (F. H. Mattern Construction Co.), and the Sherman Residence (F. H. Mattern Construction Co.), are entirely of reinforced concrete. If one takes into account the population of Tulsa at the time (which was 141,750 in 1940), these nine Streamline Art Deco houses indicate much more than a normal commitment on Tulsa's part to the imagery of the future.

The episodes of the Art Deco in Tulsa provide us with not only a sense of the universality of this imagery during the twenties and thirties, but also help us sense how individual each urban environment was in adopting it. Though all of the usual ingredients of the Art Deco styles are present in Tulsa's buildings — the way they were designed, and above all the totality of them as a group, is particular to the place. When we see the work of such strong personalities as Frank Lloyd Wright, Bruce Goff and Barry Byrne within the context of Tulsa in the mid to late twenties, their designs become more understandable. The strong individuality of their buildings remain, but it is apparent that they are in fact variations on the then popular Zigzag Art Deco. If we wish to understand how people responded to the Art Deco at that moment in history we must sense the totality of architectural imagery, which they were then experiencing. The Art Deco modes in their turn become comprehensible when we place them within the context of the predominant traditional Period architecture, and the avant-garde movement of the Modern and of Expressionism. Architecture always reveals intent: intent upon the part of the public, the specific client, and of the architect. The Art Deco buildings of Tulsa which follow should provide us with a sense of that intent.

▼
▼

ZIGZAG

"It is chiefly by private, not by public,
effort that your city
must be adorned."

— John Ruskin

Tulsa's modern skyline rises in sharp contrast to its gently rolling hills. It tells a story of the early days of "Tulsey Town," a Creek Indian village at the end of the "Trail of Tears," contrasted with the city's identity as "Oil Capital of the World." For the Indians it is a tale of treachery, of yet another broken treaty with the white man. For the white man it is the story of oil and exciting gusher wells.

Modern Tulsa dates from the 1880's when the white settlers in their steady move West began once again to encroach on the Indian lands. The treaty that declared the lands Indian Territory for "as long as the sun rises . . . as long as the waters run . . . as long as grass grows . . ." was broken with Oklahoma's statehood in 1907, a scant five years after the discovery of oil in Red Fork (now West Tulsa), and only a year after the famous Glenn Pool oil discovery ten miles south of Red Fork.[1]

By 1915, Oklahoma was the leader in the oil producing states, and Tulsa, with no oil of its own, was well on its way to becoming a major city. Starting with little more than a three-story hotel which served good meals and had a bathtub, aggressive Tulsans set out to win over the oil men. Leaders persuaded the railroads to link Tulsa with the Glenn and Cushing oil pools and with the refineries in Kansas. Free construction sites were made available to refineries and to tool manufacturers. Banks were established and oil men were chosen as directors. Promoters got preferential treatment. A good geology report was acceptable as collateral for a man who wanted to sink a well. Officials were familiar with lease and security values. The Tulsa bankers' willingness to stake wild ventures paid. The oil men came to Tulsa to do their banking. Many chose to live there because it was a nice place for their families but not too far removed from the drilling.

The lavish spirit of the oil industry affected civic planning. Tulsans used their money as dramatically, and often as fast, as they acquired it. The prevalent attitude of the oil men toward their money seemed to be, "easy come, easy go." They were very generous to the city. Oil man William G. Skelly was fond of saying, "What's good for Tulsa is good for me." They did not place much emphasis on ownership, but on monuments for remembering.

These men were as enamored of the gambling and uncertainty as they were of the money or the oil. They were reckless, extravagant, and daring. Thomas B. Slick, a lease promoter for a Chicago financier and lifetime friend of Skelly's, typifies this special breed. Slick paid one dollar per acre for leases within a ten-mile radius of a discovery well at Cushing in 1912. To keep the strike a secret while he played his game of monopoly, he hired all the livery rigs in Cushing and paid the town's notaries to take the day off, so that no one else could file a claim. His ingenuity characterized the Oklahoma oil barons. Is it any wonder that this go-for-broke attitude would build in a carefree decorative style?

By the 20's Tulsa had come of age as the "Oil Capital of the World." The first International Petroleum Exposition was held in 1923. Oil men and their money flowed into Tulsa. Easterners, attracted by stories of black gold, made the city an important part of their itinerary. Some stayed, impressing the Southwesterners with their eastern culture and sophisticated ways. Young people from the East gave Tulsa a different atmosphere. The resultant social and cultural whirl set in motion lots of parties, lots of drinking, and lots of divorce. This frivolity, coupled with the oil money gushing into Tulsa, made it a very exuberant place.

The 20's in Tulsa was a time of unparalleled growth as it was across the country. The population in Tulsa virtually doubled. Buildings were under construction to house the businesses that were drawing people to Tulsa. By 1927 the downtown was enjoying a building boom of $1 million a month, every month. Downtown was a cacophony of building sounds. Rivots were not welded in those days; they were beaten in. The sound was deafening. The noise made it almost impossible to hold classes in the downtown Central High School. The skyline, webbed with steel framing and scaffolding, looked like a child's erector set. By the end of the decade Tulsa had more "skyscrapers" (buildings at least ten-stories high) than any other city of its size in the world. The cluster and balance of Tulsa's skyline, that some have called "almost European," is a result of that rapid growth and of the unity of the forces that produced it.

Tulsans in the early 20's were torn between being imitators and being innovators. The lack of roots in any indigenous architectural tradition left Tulsans free to experiment. But they were apologetic for their city's lack of that history and permanence which characterized the eastern cities they had left. The temptation in the early 20's, when Tulsans began to build a great city, was to acquire tradition by emulating it. In architecture, Gothic was de rigueur. It was the style of Europe. It was the style of the churches.

The buildings in the first half of the decade illustrated the predisposition toward the traditional and conservative. By the latter half of the decade, however, the pioneer passion to explore new horizons can be seen in the architecture. Coinciding with Tulsa's frenetic building boom a jazzy, popular "modern" look was gaining favor in Europe as well as in the United States. Tulsans embraced it. This was the popular style we have come to call "Art Deco."

Art Deco derived its name and its sanction from the 1925 Paris Exposition, "L'Exposition Internationale des Arts Decoratifs et Industriels Modernes." As its name would imply, at that time it was an ornamental style. It was *haut monde,* ultrasophisticated, and intended for the very few who could afford such lavishness. The original style was a designer style, one that made extravagant use of the finest materials. In the decorative arts and in furniture design, ivory and ebony and the most exotic inlays and lacquers were favored. Architectural richness included elaborate ornamentation and materials such as bronze, copper, and the new alloys with their shimmering metallic look; etched and sandblasted glass; polished granite, marble, onyx, and terra cotta.

Art Deco borrowed unabashedly. Its introduction into the Parisian imagination probably dates as early as 1909 with the arrival of Diaghilev and his Ballet Russe. They exploded on the Parisian consciousness with a boldness of color in costume and set design that made the delicate tendrils of the Art Nouveau period pale by comparison. The dramatic stage sets were borrowed from the theater by Deco designers. The opening of Tutankhamen's tomb in 1922 popularized Egyptian art. Deco designers borrowed from it. The Mexican Revolution focused attention on Mexico and the Mayan designs. Deco borrowed from them. The art of the North and South American Indians provided a fertile source for Deco designs. The borrowings were eclectic, dipping into Cubism, Fauvism, and Expressionism. Such eclecticism condensed European architectural history into a package, a ready-made "tradition" appealing to a city in a hurry for a big city identity. Tulsa asserted itself in the 20's, through its architecture, as a city with ties to other national and international cities.

If a decade could be reduced to a geometric form, then the shape of the 20's would be that of a soaring vertical line, and the direction would be up. It was a time of optimism. The war to end all wars had been fought and won. The tempo was jazz. It was George Gershwin and "Rhapsody in Blue." The stock market skyrocketed to new heights, as did personal wealth, at least on paper. It was a frivolous and flamboyant time, a time of wonderful nonsense.

The terms "Zigzag Art Deco" and "Skyscraper Style" are sometimes used interchangeably. Verticality was the emphasis of the soaring 20's. Tall buildings were made to look taller. A common device was the use of piers rising without interruption from the second floor to the top of the building. Window treatment was another artiface used to create a vertical look. Windows were run in vertical strips using spandrels of a dark material or heavy texture. An illusion was created of windows and spandrels set in one continuous line to the apex of the building.

The typical Zigzag building was arranged in a series of set backs, culminating in a tower. The building itself was shaped like a ziggurat (a stepped pyramid), a preeminent Deco form, both ornamentally and structurally. The Empire State Building and the RCA Building in Rockefeller Center are arranged in the ziggurat form.

Other recurring Deco designs were the fountain, the chevron, the sun and its rays. Exotic scenes followed exotic designs and materials. Jungles of animals were portrayed from snakes and lizards to deer, greyhounds, rabbits, and all sorts of birds, particularly the eagle. Symbols of energy, the lightning bolt (a ziggurat shape), stepped triangles, fragmented circles, and spirals were commonly used.

Deco was a mood, a stage set. The "jazz age" was transposed to ornamentation. Details repeated the buildings' themes in ornamentation. Designs were consistent inside and out, even to the doorknobs and grilles over heat registers. Elevators and lobbies were turned into twentieth century art forms. It was a time of splendor and fantasy.

At the same time a more serious architecture was developing called the International Style. It was esoteric, an architecture of functionalism. Architectural purists, Le Corbusier (who protested the 1925 Paris Exhibition), Mies van der Rohe and Walter Gropius, considered the popular Art Deco a commercial prostitution. Proportion, not ornament, was their god. Engineering technology and building materials were to be the determining factors in the design of a building, and efficiency the keynote to planning. Desirable qualities were simplicity and clarity. A schism developed between these two camps. International Style architects scorned Art Deco as the illegitimate cousin.

Art Deco won some of the major battles for public acceptance in the 20's and 30's, but ultimately lost the war. In fact, its very popularity, its acceptance by the uncultured masses, doomed it with the elite. Looking across the country today it is apparent that the real architectural revolution of the twentieth century has been the work of the International Style. A depression and a Second World War added a sobering mood consistent with that style's austerity. Ornament appeared giddy. People felt the need to strip their buildings as they had stripped the non-essentials from their lives. "Doing without," an established practice in the Depression, became a way of life during the rationing of World War II. The new buildings too were designed to reflect the austerity.

Art Deco arrived in Tulsa in 1927, among flapper skirts and high divorce rates, just in time to be commemorated in the downtown building boom. A fanciful and whimsical style, a theatrical look, Art Deco was a reflection of the mood of the twenties.

The colorful and ornamental Art Deco Zigzag Style was made possible in part by the popular use of terra cotta as a sheathing material. Terra cotta, Latin for "burnt earth," first achieved wide use as a building material for its excellent fireproofing qualities. Pursuant to the new fire codes, it was used extensively in Chicago after the Great Fire of 1871. Architects also discovered that terra cotta had other structural advantages in the building of skyscrapers. It was light, durable, and seemed to have infinite possibilities for decorative uses. The weight of terra cotta was one half that of stone, because terra cotta blocks were hollow to facilitate firing. "Above all, its plastic qualities enabled architects to use terra cotta to embellish their structures with artistic and highly original ornament."[2]

Terra cotta's popularity as an ornamental building material peaked in the late 20's as did Tulsa's great downtown building boom. By 1920 the terra cotta industry had become standardized and mechanized. No longer did the laborer's bare feet mix the water into the powdered clay substance as they had done the preceeding century. Now machines crushed and ground and moved the clay. Northwestern Terra Cotta Company of Chicago, the largest terra cotta factory in the nation, had railroad tracks on which terra cotta blocks were inched along in train carloads to bake slowly for a week in a 400 foot tunnel kiln. The chemistry of ceramics became more sophisticated, and tens of thousands of glaze formulas were available, with colors ranging from the standard commercial buff to glittering ceramic gold.

By this time too the terra cotta companies had a backlog of molds representing forty or even fifty years of modeling. Recognizing the importance of remaining competitive as a material supplier, they made stock designs available through catalogues. Ornamentation could be ordered by number much as one might make a mail order purchase. An architect could flip through a large catalogue, pick out spandrels, piers, pinnacles, in fact his whole building facade, and know the exact price and the exterior weight that the structure would be required to bear. By choosing a catalogue design instead of commissioning custom work, he could save the cost of a modeler.

Factory workers arranged each piece of terra cotta in the order that it was to be put on the building and numbered the pieces in sequence. When the terra cotta arrived at the building site, it was stacked in the pre-assigned numerical order. It was then hung like a picture on the building's framework and grouted in place.

At the beginning of Tulsa's downtown boom, designs in a new style of ornamentation had reached the terra cotta industry. These were "modern French" motifs inspired in part by designs from the dazzling Paris Exposition of 1925. Northwestern Terra Cotta Company, eager to capitalize on the popularity of the French designs, hired six French modelers to work in its factory. Borrowing designs from the large Exposition catalogues, the six modelers captivated the public fancy with the new "Art Deco" or "moderne." "Soon colorful stylized flowers, dancing zigzags, plump birds, and exotic maidens began to make their debut . . . ."[3]

Terra cotta's popularity, the impact of the modern French designs, and Tulsa's downtown building frenzy all coincided and coalesced. Tulsa became a veritable rhapsody of ziggurats and chevrons, zigzags and lightning bolts, fountains and sunbursts, gods and goddesses, Gauguin jungles with lurking animals amidst the flora, all of this on spandrels and between pinnacles, over doorways and under cornices, and all in terra cotta. So much so that by the end of the 20's, those in the terra cotta industry had dubbed Tulsa "Terra Cotta City."

Terra cotta had been used extensively in Tulsa in the early 20's, but its ornamentation had been of Gothic design. It was not until 1927 that the architectural firm of Arthur M. Atkinson completed the eleven-story Medical and Dental Arts building, and in so doing, initiated Tulsa into the Zigzag Art Deco, and into the Art Deco use of terra cotta. The three earliest Art Deco buildings in Tulsa came from Atkinson's office.

Arthur M. Atkinson (1891-1949) was a registered professional engineer as well as architect, an expert on modern lighting techniques, and has been referred to as the first modernistic architect in Tulsa. Atkinson's office, the largest in Tulsa in the 20's, operated at a hectic pace. His method for turning out a job was the charrette, and all of his employees became adept at all-out, all-night labors when a deadline loomed. But Atkinson's employees also remember that he balanced work with play. In the summer after an all night session he would often tell his staff to get some sleep and come back with their bathing suits for some fun.

Atkinson was content to turn over the exterior design work to others, but he would critique the designs and make suggestions. His joy was in the electrical work. Rotating in and out of Atkinson's office in the 20's were two young architects, Joseph R. Koberling, Jr. (1900-   ), and Frederick Vance Kershner (1904-1980).

Koberling, schooled in Chicago, felt that his classmates at Armour Institute were beginning to develop a sense of "American Expressionism" and an identity with "our era." While in Chicago he met both Louis Sullivan and

1928 RENDERING BY JOSEPH R. KOBERLING, JR.

Eliel Saarinen and was very much influenced by their work. He described Saarinen's second place Tribune Tower design for the Tribune Competition of 1922 as "poetic—a series of lines reaching for the sky." His profound feeling for this work is later expressed in the lines of the Medical and Dental Arts Building and in the facade of the Genet Building in Tulsa.

Koberling took a year off to go to Europe (1927-1928) on a traveling scholarship to study the various European architectural movements. He toured England, Wales, Germany, Switzerland, France, and Spain. He was repelled by the "soulless architecture" of the then contemporary German Bauhaus style. "It was," he said, "so against the traditional joyfulness of architecture."

Kershner also traveled in Europe. He attended the Ecole des Beaux Arts in Fontainebleau, France, his studies overlapping the period of Koberling's travels abroad. Unlike Koberling, he was impressed by the International Bauhaus Style.

The Medical and Dental Arts Building, 6th Street and Boulder Avenue, was eleven stories with a full basement. Designed by Joseph Koberling, Jr. while he was employed by Atkinson, it was built for Dr. Charles W. Day, a dentist. Although the building retained some elements of the Gothic influence, it broke with the past in favor of the Zigzag Art Deco style. Its terra cotta ornament was custom-made by Northwestern Terra Cotta of Chicago and sheathed the building in the linear skyscraper style. The terra cotta was ivory, set off with dark green spandrels, further emphasizing the verticality of the building. The ivory piers terminated as ziggurats. A Gothic influence appeared in the arches that were repeated on the main floor and top floor of the building. A neo-Gothic frieze ornamented the building at the roof line.

The structure fulfilled Dr. Day's dream of constructing a beautiful downtown building to house the medical and dental professions. He had traveled extensively across the country to inspect buildings of this type for innovative ideas to incorporate into his building. The interior of the building, for example, was custom designed for each doctor's office. The prospective tenants made appointments with Atkinson's office, so that their space requirements would be met. There was a clubroom and a library in the basement for the use of the professionals in the building.

Tulsans liked the Medical Arts Building and it was a tremendous success. It was, as Day had anticipated, THE home for the medical profession in Tulsa. Dr. Day was able to enjoy his new office building for only a few years. He died January 2, 1934. Two years after his death his building was foreclosed on and sold. It continued to function as a medical building, but the lack of central air-conditioning and a mass exit of clients to the suburbs doomed the building to destruction in later years.

Tulsa's next two Zigzag Art Deco buildings were built for utility companies. The Oklahoma Natural Gas Company and the Public Service Company of Oklahoma, gas and electric utilities respectively, both invested in downtown buildings in the late 20's. The utilities were attracted to Tulsa by its mushrooming growth. Tulsa's potential as a major city had lured Oklahoma Natural Gas to move its home offices from Oklahoma City to Tulsa in 1926.

Both utility company buildings were on the drawing boards at the same time in Atkinson's office, and their exteriors look related. Both are buff colored and have traditionally Gothic main floors, with the Art Deco influences above the main floor in the vertical accents of the buildings. Koberling attributes the similarities of the buildings to the "spirit of the artist." He designed the exterior of the Oklahoma Natural Gas Building before he left for his year abroad, and his friend Kershner completed the design. When he returned from Europe, Koberling designed the Public Service Company Building.

The Oklahoma Natural Gas Building, completed in 1928, at a cost of $600,000, is ten-stories with a basement. Constructed of reinforced concrete, and enclosed with buff-tapestry brick, it is trimmed with Indiana limestone

EXTERIOR CIRCA 1930

and vitreus tile.

The Public Service Company Building constructed a year later, and costing $425,000 was five stories with a basement and a foundation for an additional three stories. Two more floors were added in 1961.

The building is also of reinforced concrete, but covered by buff Bedford stone instead of brick. The Public Service Company Building was designed to feature exterior lighting, a dictum from the company officials. Since they were in the business of lighting, it was effective advertising for their building to be dramatically illuminated at night. To meet the requirement, flood lights were recessed in insets at the second floor and at the top levels of the building. In the beginning colored lights were used year around to create sensational displays. Atkinson's reputation as an expert on modern lighting originated with the Public Service Company Building.

The adoption of the new Art Deco style by the somewhat conservative utility companies ushered in a new era for Tulsa building. Any lingering doubts about Art Deco's acceptance were dispelled by the construction of Tulsa's pioneer department store, Halliburton-Abbott. It incorporated all the elements of the Zigzag Art Deco.

A seven-story building was constructed for the Halliburton-Abbott department store. It included a mezzanine, a basement thrift shop, and a foundation that could support an additional five floors. The structure had a linear quality similar to that found in the architecture of Barry Byrne, the Chicago modernist, and of Bruce Goff. It appeared as a solid base with the building rising above it. The terrazzo base anchored the building while terra cotta piers set in vertical projections soared above it. The facade of the building was arranged in a series of set backs, with the roof line suggesting Medieval pinnacles. Recessed between the parapets were polychrome Mayan terra cotta moldings—a flat French moderne touch—by Northwestern Terra Cotta's St. Louis factory. The moldings included rosettes, chevrons, and scroll-like designs in repeating panels of gold, blue, red, and green.

The building was faced with buff terra cotta ashlars. Ashlars are uniform blocks, made and glazed to resemble different types of stone. The art of glazing had become so sophisticated in the terra cotta industry that literally any type of stone could be imitated. The imitations were so convincing that one still had to tap the building's facade to determine by sound and feel whether it was stone or terra cotta.

BRONZE ELEVATOR DOORS

CENTRAL HALL CEILING DETAIL

NIGHT LIGHTING CIRCA 1950

EXTERIOR CIRCA 1930

EXTERIOR TERRA COTTA AT ROOFLINE

The windows accented the building's verticality by occurring as an element of the recessed panels. The spandrels were decorated with a chevron design, a design repeated in wrought iron over the entry and at the base of the mezzanine windows. The glass in the mezzanine windows was etched in a scroll pattern. A horizontal band of geometric ornamentation capped the mezzanine floor, the same geometric designs that were found inside decorating the cross beams on the first floor and repeated in the ornamental plaster bordering the ceilings.

The beginnings of the Halliburton-Abbott department store were humble, its history very much intermingled with the history of Tulsa itself. Even before Tulsa was named or platted, "Has" Reed and Joshua Perryman, a Creek Indian, founded a store on the east side of the Arkansas River at the future site of the Frisco Railroad Bridge. Unfortunately, the Frisco Railroad, then under construction, stopped short of their store. In 1882, Reed and Perryman moved their location to First and Main Streets in order to be closer to the railhead. Four years later they sold their interest. The store changed ownership several more times until in 1916 the Halliburton-Abbott Company bought it from Harlow Dry Goods. In less than two years Halliburton-Abbott found itself too cramped in its three-story structure at 3rd and Boston, and moved to a five-story building at 5th and Main Streets. In so doing, Halliburton-Abbott became the first to expand the downtown shopping area south as far as 5th Street. It was appropriate that Halliburton-Abbott, a pioneer in a pioneer city, should continue to play a leading part in the direction of the city's growth as well as of the city's new architecture.

Nineteen twenty-nine found Halliburton-Abbott moving and expanding again. When L. E. Abbott, head of the company, decided upon plans for the new seven-story building he had only one instruction for architect Frank C. Walter (1870-1953). The tone was Tulsa booster and Oklahoma proud. If possible, all materials, products, and labor were to be from Tulsa. In no case were any of the three to come from outside Oklahoma. In every instance Tulsa contractors were to be given preference over all others. In fulfilling these priorities, it was felt that the new building would be one indication of Tulsa's burgeoning industrial development.

The building was praised as being "the finest structure of its kind in the Southwest and the most modern in conception and equipment."[4] The 1929 *Tulsa World* newspaper articles for November 24 and December 1 describing the building gave an impression of its impact:

> When the guests enter the big doors a week from next Monday night they will walk into a great room whose first impression is one of space and harmony. The lines, the design and the coloring of the room and its adornment are quiet and in excellent taste.
> The great lights [descending] from the high ceiling are plain as lamps can be. But they are of daring modernistic design. Crystal and silver and the soft light and the bold design of the lamp itself immediately catch and hold the eye.
> The design of the ornamental plaster around the foot of the balcony is in soft colors and its lines are excellent. In the display window . . . is a big round fountain.
> Lining the north and south (of the 3rd floor) are the fitting rooms, each one an exquisite little setting for lovely frocks and lovely women. One is orchid, another rose, another a pale green, another a dull gold, another blue. She, with a sensitive feeling for color, may harmonize room with frock if she likes!

The building did have a number of innovations for its time. It was the first department store in Oklahoma to be centrally air-conditioned. The basement thrift store was new to Tulsa, and the elevators, although still manned by operators, were self-stopping with automatic floor leveling. A tunnel under 5th Street connected Halliburton-Abbott to the Mayo Furniture Store.

The store's grand opening was held Monday night, December 2, 1929 . . . less than five weeks after the stock market crash and twelve years before Pearl Harbor. An era had ended but the reaction would be a delayed one. Nothing would ever be quite the same. But for Tulsa and for most of the rest of the country, it was still the

PLASTER CAPITAL DETAIL

PLASTER MOLDING DETAIL

PLASTER BEAM DETAIL

CEILING AIR VENT

frivolous, fabulous 20's.

Priding itself as a pacesetter in style, Halliburton-Abbott launched the opening of its new store with an advertising campaign that was itself a pacesetter. The store advertised heavily in the Sunday *Tulsa World* the day before the opening with a thirty-two page section of ads devoted exclusively to the store's opening and set a new record for newspaper advertising by a department store.

The ads tell us a lot about the times. If there is a recurring theme, it is "new and Modern." There is an emphasis on "total costuming," with New York and Paris constantly referred to in the ads as the fashion leaders. Anything with that geographical stamp of approval was the ultimate in vogue. "Costumes of the highest type, as smart as those of gay Parisians and sophisticated New Yorkers . . . ."

"As modern as tomorrow," "the modernism of youth," the woman as "the moderne" were all catch advertising phrases. There was a new silhouette for the modern woman. It was, as today, slim.

Aviation suits for "today's woman" appeared in the ads. It was important to be correctly "costumed" for flying. The new excitement about air travel and the impact of Amelia Earhart as a female aviator were all depicted.

The advertising campaign, if measured by the attendance at the store's preview opening, was overwhelmingly successful. The *Tulsa World's* title story the following day was "Crowds Throng Aisles as New Store is Opened." The article continued, ". . . for there were thousands." The four passenger elevators were so taxed that the freight elevators were called into service. From the mezzanine "the main floor looked like a checkerboard of hats . . . (and) the 'strolling musicians' did valiant battle to accomplish the strolling."

Mr. and Mrs. Harry C. Tyrrell attended the opening. Tyrrell, as a partner in the Boulder Building Corporation with J. M. Gillette, Cass A. Mayo, and John D. Mayo, was part owner of the Halliburton-Abbott Building, which the department store leased. Tyrrell had a peripheral interest as well. He was also part owner, with J. M. Gillette, of another building in the process of construction just diagonally across the intersection.

J. M. Gillette and Harry C. Tyrrell were both Tulsa oil men and financiers. Their three-story building, originally named the Gillette-Tyrrell Building, was completed in 1930. Edward W. Saunders (1878-1964) designed

WROUGHT IRON RAILING 5TH STREET ENTRANCE

ETCHED GLASS ABOVE 5TH STREET ENTRANCE

1929 RENDERING BY EDWARD W. SAUNDERS

EAST-WEST HALL

TERRA COTTA PINNACLES

CANOPY AT 5th STREET ENTRANCE

PLASTER CEILING DETAIL

CERAMIC TILE WAINSCOT

it as a thirteen-story structure with a hotel occupying the top ten floors. With the effects of the Depression that hotel space never got beyond the drawing board stage.

One of the building's original tenants, Western Union Telegraph, still has its main office on the first floor. Other first floor tenants were the Trimble Flower Shop and the French Boot Shop, along with various clothing and specialty shops. The second floor provided space for shops and offices. The third floor housed Western Union's equipment, while the basement provided cold fur storage.

The three-story Gillette-Tyrrell building, despite its basic box-like volume, appears to have the towering height of the thirteen-story building that it was intended to be. The verticality is articulated by a thin, linear skin of cream colored terra cotta. Playing on the skyscraper theme, the terra cotta facade was formed into a series of narrow vertical piers running without interruption to the top of the building. The piers are ornamented with back-to-back diamond patterns, or "dancing zigzags," a motif thoroughly explored at the French Exposition. Segmented blue terra cotta accents the spandrels and the top of the first story. The roof line, in colors of blue, tan, and green terra cotta, gives the impression of rising without termination, consistent with the original design. An anachronism is contained in the touch of the late English Gothic blue transom windows in this otherwise Zigzag Art Deco building.

Probably the most notable Art Deco feature is the L-shaped lobby, colorfully tiled in burnt siennas, green, and Roman blue. The exterior geometric patterns are repeated in the interior ornament. The tiled floor has an Indian blanket pattern, or pre-Columbian flavor, that is reflected in the bright colors painted on the geometrically carved plaster ceiling. The tile extends as wainscoting halfway up the interior walls. Above the wainscoting are windows that open into the lobby for ventilation. The glass in the windows is ornamented with a sand-blasted pattern. Long modern light fixtures, formed of prism-shaped pieces of etched glass, hang from the lobby ceiling. The fixtures were custom-made by Empire Chandelier Manufacturing Company of Sand Springs, Oklahoma. Additional elevator space was allocated in the lobby for the future ten stories.

The ten stories never materialized. Nineteen thirty-one was a difficult time for the corners of 5th and Boulder. Gillette, who had invested heavily in the stock market, was badly hurt by the crash. Tyrrell, an independent oil man, fared somewhat better. Both needed to divest, however. In December, 1931, Gillette and Tyrrell bowed out, selling to the Knights of Pythias. The building is better known as the "Pythian." Several months before, and less than two years after their gala opening, Halliburton-Abbott had been forced to give up the lease on their building. Sears, Roebuck and Company took over the lease and stayed until 1958. The building became known as the Sears Building.

The French influence, so prevalent in the Terra Cotta industry during the 20's also extended to lighting fixtures, ornamental glass and metal work. Much of Tulsa's custom modern lighting came from Empire Chandelier Manufacturing Company, located in Sand Springs, and started in 1926 by W. J. Smiley, president. Empire's fixtures lit the Philtower, the Medical and Dental Arts Building, the Gillette-Tyrrell (Pythian) Building, the Riverside Studio, Christ the King Church, and many other Tulsa buildings.

Smiley was said to have begun his company with "an artistic temperament and a burning ambition in the way of equipment."[5] He prided himself on employing craftsmen and he paid them accordingly. His artists drew the highest average wages of any industrial payroll in the state. One of his designers and draftsmen was Lawrence Loftus, a Frenchman, who could be found in Smiley's work area reading the trade journal from Paris, "La Luminaire, et les Moyens d'Eclairages."

Special glass work such as etched, engraved, beveled, and silvered glass was provided by Ornamental Glass Company. They too employed European craftsmen. Because etching glass was a slow and laborious process, much of the glass in Tulsa buildings in the 20's was sandblasted by the Tulsa Monument Company.

In the first quarter of the 20th century, Edgar Brandt, a Parisian, broadened the scope of ironwork and its decorative usage. His entirely original approach resulted in a wrought-iron texture that resembled beaten silver. His work, exhibited at the 1925 Paris Exposition of Decorative Arts had an immediate effect upon ironwork designed and executed in the United States during the great building boom that lasted until the Depression.

Wrought iron is fibrous, and when hot, it is soft enough to be easily modeled and shaped. Separate pieces weld perfectly if they are hammered together. The more the iron is worked, the greater its strength and toughness when cool.

Many of the tools and techniques used in the forging process differed little from those used in medieval times. The medieval forge, dependent upon hand or foot operated bellows to keep the draught flowing, had been replaced by an electrically powered machine. This draught flow was necessary to produce the intense heat required to make the iron flexible.

In Tulsa during the 20's and 30's hand forging was rare. Most of the ironwork was cast or made from molds. Wrought iron was still very expensive, and casting cut the cost considerably. Metal work in Tulsa was produced by Tulsa Ornamental Iron Company, Tulsa Iron and Wire Works, and Empire Chandelier Manufacturing Company. Empire's custom metal work included ornamental iron grilles, ballustrades, bronze, brass and aluminum castings.

But Tulsa craftsmen did not have the facilities for large items. The canopies so prevalent during the era of Art Deco probably came from architectural metal shops in Philadelphia. These enormous canopies, also called porte cocheres, were status symbols to match the status symbol of the then novel automobile. They were placed on the front of the building for the convenience of the automobile passenger who could disembark at the door without being exposed to the elements. Where there were canopies, there were often doormen. Most of the downtown Deco buildings of the 20's had a canopy at the front entrance, and corner buildings often had a front and a side canopy.

While Halliburton-Abbott and the Gillette-Tyrrell buildings were projected for the new, smart shopping area of 5th and Boulder, the Bliss Hotel was under construction several blocks north, closer to the site where excavation was about to begin for the Union Train Depot.

The erection of the Bliss Hotel was a microcosm of the frantic building activity occurring in Tulsa in 1928. Ground was broken on September 1, 1928, and the 140' x 69' structure with ten stories and a basement was completed just eight months later. The hotel had 225 rooms, each with an outside exposure, and all equipped with bath, shower, and circulating ice water. The building cost $600,000, the furnishings $100,000, and the site $150,000, a total cost of $850,000.

The hotel was built for Charles Bliss, a lawyer, oil man, and entrepreneur, whose father had owned hotels in Missouri and Kansas. Bliss had come to Oklahoma in 1904 to practice law in Muskogee. It was a propitious decision, for among his early clients were Galbreath and Chesley, the men who discovered the famous Glenn Pool oil field in Tulsa County. Bliss's interest in oil investments and property soon superceeded his interest in the law. While still practicing, he founded the Bliss Drilling Company and associated with his father in building the Bliss Office Building in Tulsa. Charles Bliss moved to Tulsa in 1914. The following year he organized the Bliss Oil and Gas Company with a refinery in Augusta, Kansas.

Arriving as he did to play a part in Tulsa's rapid growth, Bliss could see the need for more hotel space. That, coupled with an urge to re-enter the business in which he had grown up, led to the Bliss Hotel. He first considered converting the existing Bliss Office Building into a hotel, but finally decided to erect a new structure at 2nd Street and Boston Avenue.

Bliss chose Leland I. Shumway (1891-1969), often referred to as the "School Architect," to design the hotel. Shumway served as the architect for the Tulsa Board of Education in the 20's and 30's and designed over thirteen schools in Tulsa during that time. But building hotels was not new to him; he was the architect for four hotels in downtown Tulsa and one in Oklahoma City.

The Bliss Hotel was faced with buff colored brick and cream colored glazed terra cotta. The ornamentation played between the historic and the Art Deco. Terra cotta was employed to provide a classically articulated main entrance. It was Art Deco in the vertical accent of its brick piers and recessed windows. Just below the tenth story, a ribbon of terra cotta, broken in a Zigzag Art Deco mode, reinforced the upward movement of the eye. Eagles capped the parapet. The terra cotta ornamentation was designed by Harry B. Blue (1895-   ), while he was working for Shumway.

The Blisses were both very active in their support of the opera, and many visiting musicians stayed at the Bliss Hotel. Lily Pons, the famed soprano from the Metropolitan Opera, was a good friend of the Bliss family. She stayed at the hotel so often that a suite on the fifth floor was named "The Lily Pons Suite." Rose Brampton, another Met star, was also a guest at the Bliss.

Although well patronized, the hotel fell victim to the Depression and was forced into receivership in 1933. In October, 1936, with the aid of a $200,000 loan from the Reconstruction Finance Corporation, the hotel was regained by the original owners. It remained in the Bliss family until 1960.

Across the street from the Bliss Hotel, T. E. Genet once again found himself outgrowing his space. He had come to Tulsa in the early 1900's and started a furniture store in a small room on 2nd Street. Genet Furniture Store expanded with Tulsa, and by the end of the 20's, business was so good that Genet felt the need to open a second furniture store in the downtown area. The second store was twelve stories.

The first three floors were balconied for showroom display. The entire eleventh floor provided meeting facilities

EXTERIOR CIRCA 1950 (BLISS)

EXTERIOR CIRCA 1953 (GENET)

for Tulsa women's organizations. Included was an auditorium with a seating capacity of approximately 400. Chairs could be removed for dancing or for the popular bridge games. Genet's offered all this as a courtesy to the Tulsa women. The top floor contained a restaurant and club operated separately by Herb Henrici.

Built by the architect Noble Fleming (1892-1937), the front facade of the building was designed by a moonlighting Joseph Koberling. Genet's facade was buff terra cotta similar in design to that of the Medical Arts Building. The segmented arches at ground level were Gothic in feeling, but the linear piers and strong verticality indicated the Art Deco.

Genet's had been a thriving business. The store carried a wide range of furniture, from the very expensive to the modestly priced. There was a department of interior decoration headed by Malcolm Johnson. Two floors of the new store were devoted to shops that made draperies, carpets, and shades. These shops also did upholstering, furniture finishing, and cabinet work.

Genet remembered starting his furniture business with "$1,500, one man, and a black horse for deliveries. I was bookkeeper, cabinet maker, and janitor."[6] He credited the movies with "creating a demand for good furniture . . . (People) see beautiful furniture in the pictures and want it in their homes."

In an interview at the time that his new store opened in 1930, Genet said that he would have been wiser to have expanded sooner. He had underestimated Tulsa's rapid growth. How much wiser he would have been, he was soon to discover. Within two years he had lost his new store. The property was sold for $200,000.

There was at least one man in Tulsa who could afford to ignore the Depression, and that man was Waite Phillips, for Waite Phillips had the Midas touch. Phillips came to Oklahoma from the coal business in Iowa to join his brothers, Frank and Lee, who were developing oil properties in Bartlesville. He was not happy working for another man, particularly his older brother, Frank, with whom he felt some rivalry, so he set out on his own. In 1915 he began operations in Okmulgee County and within a few months he made his first strike. Almost overnight he became a millionaire. His successes multiplied during the oil boom accompanying World War I, and by the end of the war he was regarded as one of the leading oil men in the West. In 1924 he sold his oil properties for $5 million. Just one year later, in 1925, he sold his new holdings for $25 million. Discontented, he formed yet another company in 1926, and by 1929 Waite Phillips was a major figure in Tulsa's philanthropic and business communities. He had erected the Philtower Office Building on the northeast corner of 5th Street and Boston Avenue and was in the process of constructing an annex across the street from the Philtower that would become known as the Philcade.

When Waite Phillips built the twenty-four-story ornately Gothic Philtower Office Building in 1927, he took the precaution of purchasing the tract of land to the south, site of the old Boston Avenue Methodist Church. It was, and is, a common practice to acquire, and thus control the quality of the site opposite the entrance of such a major building if that site is not already developed. At the time Phillips had no plans for the property. However, everything changed abruptly in the fall of 1928 when he discovered that a number of Main Street merchants' leases were about to expire and that they were being approached by certain business interests to relocate on Boulder Avenue. Phillips viewed this prospect with alarm. If the merchants moved west, the direction of growth would be away from the Philtower, and Phillips's property would be jeopardized.

By the time Halliburton-Abbott had located at the corner of 5th and Boulder, ambitious Tulsans were intent upon changing 5th "Street" to 5th "AVENUE" in order to emulate stylish New York. Phillips was very much in favor of the "5th Avenue" movement because 5th Street or "5th Avenue" came in the side door of the Philtower. The name change never caught on, but the Street, even as "5th Street" became a desired retail location. Main Street between 4th and 5th was the principal shopping area and was therefore the most sought after as a location by

FIFTH STREET ELEVATION

SCALE 1/8" = 1'-0"

ORIGINAL 5TH STREET ELEVATION

5TH STREET EXTERIOR

TERRA COTTA DETAIL OVER WINDOWS

WROUGHT IRON EAGLE AND TERRA COTTA

TERRA COTTA FOUNTAIN MOTIF AT ENTRY

Tulsa merchants. The Philcade, offering new shop space and promoting Boston Avenue as the most desirable shop and office location, was a response to the threat of the westerly expansion toward Boulder.

The evolution of a major building is no casual blending of a client's money with his architect's ideas. The time the structure is to be built, its size, shape, architectural style, the materials to be used, the details of construction — all may be influenced by commercial considerations imperceptible to the public at large. Records kept of the planning meetings for the Philcade Building reveal this elusive process.

On November 26th and 27th, 1928, the Building Planning Service met in Tulsa to discuss Waite Phillips's proposed office building. This committee was a service of the National Association of Building Owners and Managers, and was composed of owners of major buildings from across the country. They came from Chicago, Kansas City, Birmingham, Omaha and St. Louis. Tulsa's representative was Noble Thompson, owner of the Thompson Building. W. Frank Walker represented Phillips, and the architectural firm of Smith and Senter, architects for the building, was represented by McIntyre, Wolaver, Taylor and Tailler.

The purpose of the Building Planning Service described at the beginning of the meeting was "an advisory committee to assist in determining whether the project under contemplation is a sound project, to avoid any errors or mistakes from making this an outstanding development, the highest type of development that can be placed on this piece of ground in Tulsa."

W. Frank Walker, speaking for Waite Phillips, stated, "We thought it necessary for the protection of Mr. Phillips's investments on Boston Avenue for the development of this building." He went on to describe the business climate in downtown Tulsa and its bearing on the decision to build the Philcade.

Waite Phillips originally specified a two-story shop building. By the time the Building Planning Service began meeting, however, the building had grown to five stories. Phillips discarded the two-story plan as looking too squatty. It was thought that although the office space might not be rented for some time, a larger building was justified for its better appearance. So from inception to final addition, the Philcade mushroomed from a modest idea to a thirteen-story reality that offered more office space than any other building in Oklahoma at that time.

Since Tulsa had a 17 per cent vacancy rate in office space in 1928, there was a risk that the Philcade would become direct competition for the Philtower. To avoid this possibility, it was decided that the Philcade should not be of a price or of a class to compete with the Philtower. Consequently, the architect, Leon Senter (1889-1965), was asked to design as modest a building as possible and still build it well.

Leon Senter and Waite Phillips met in Okmulgee when Phillips was starting his oil operations there. They were next-door neighbors. Senter was a young architect heading the Okmulgee office of Smith and Senter, a Kansas City based firm. Waite Phillips brought Leon Senter to Tulsa specifically to build the Philcade. Phillips installed Senter in his prestigious Philtower Office Building, where Senter practiced until the end of his long and successful career.

Other matters coming under discussion by the Building Planning Service were the cost and advisability of marble; the best shape for the building, an H-shape being generally favored; whether or not to use arcades; how much money to invest in the foundation with a view to future expansion; and whether to have shops or office space on the second floor.

Construction on the Philcade began in January of 1929. At that time the proposed structure was to be five floors with structural members and foundations designed to accommodate a future addition of three stories. In mid-construction the plans were redesigned for a nine-story building with allowance for a future addition of three floors. The nine-story Philcade was completed in 1930.

The biggest construction problem in the building of the Philcade was the tunnel that was to connect the

EAST-WEST HALL

NORTH-SOUTH HALL

5TH STREET ENTRANCE DETAIL

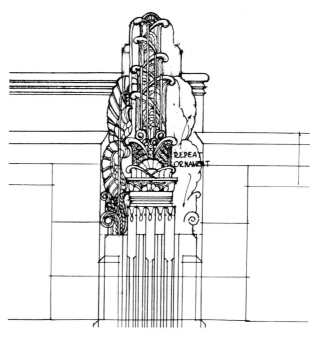

5TH STREET ENTRANCE DETAIL

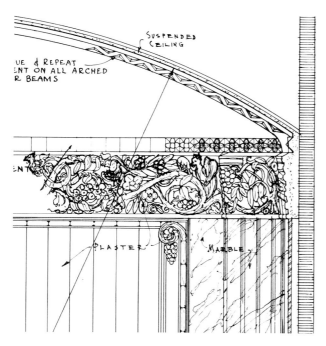

INTERIOR PLASTER ARCADE DETAIL

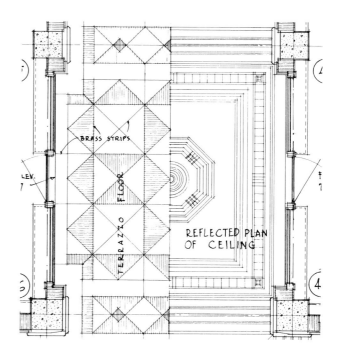

PLAN DETAIL OF ELEVATOR LOBBY

Philcade to the Philtower. Miners were imported to dig the tunnel under Boston Avenue. The 80 foot tunnel was made of brick and arched to better carry the load of the street above. The purpose of the tunnel was to provide for easy transportation of supplies from one building to the other and to make the large amount of storage space in the Philcade accessible to the Philtower as well. There was another more clandestine purpose to the tunnel. Phillips, alarmed by the recent Chicago kidnappings of wealthy oil men, wished to be able to move from building to building secretly and in relative safety, if necessary.

The Philcade opened in 1930 with 259 suites of offices and 28 shops. The very simple exterior of the Philcade, as compared to the ornate Philtower, is in keeping with the instruction given to the architect to design as modest a building as possible and still build it well. It was designed with the same colored brick as the Philtower to give the two buildings a harmonious appearance, and their 5th Street entrances were exactly aligned. In every way the Philcade was intended as a complement rather than as a challenge to the more proud Philtower.

The Philcade was described on completion as "a practical application of conservative modernistic architecture to (a) business structure."[7] The exterior of the building is vertical, and all ornamentation is without projection to minimize any expression of horizontal lines.

The first two floors are terra cotta and the roof line has terra cotta trim on its regularly spaced pinnacles. Between the pinnacles is a metalwork design that is repeated in the glass over the foyer doors. The entrances are flanked by terra cotta pilasters articulated with vertical fluting. In the entrance is a terra cotta panel of flattened fern-shaped corn sheaves reflecting the Egyptian influence often seen in Art Deco ornamentation. The building's terra cotta portrays the passion for stylized, Gauguin-shaped flora and fauna that was synonymous with flat French moderne. On close examination, the exterior terra cotta includes a zoological garden of delightful animals — rabbits, turtles, frogs, lizards, squirrels, and birds. The recurrent Deco eagles add the coup de grâce to a wrought iron floral and fish design over the large first floor windows.

The influence of the French modelers, brought to this country by Northwestern Terra Cotta of Chicago, was at its peak at the time the Philcade was being built. Their designs included the repetitive geometric shapes so well

HEAT REGISTER GRILLE

RETURN AIR GRILLE

received at the Paris Exposition of 1925. These designs were more flattened than the traditional terra cotta moldings. They relied on brilliant color and distinct form to set apart their patterns. There was a great deal of similarity between the Deco designs and those designs encountered in Post-Impressionist paintings and in some Art Nouveau decoration.

In the Art Deco tradition, an effort was made to achieve continuity between the exterior and interior of the building. The floral motif on the building's facade is carried over to the friezes in the two arcades. A fanciful touch is a floral designed wrought iron grille that covers a heat register in the foyer. Despite the instruction to the architect to design the building simply, this sort of detailing was apparently considered essential.

The H-shape of the Philcade, chosen by the Building Planning Service and allowing more light and airflow, was also the choice of the client for commercial reasons. Two 14 foot wide arcades open onto Boston Avenue and onto 5th Street, giving the Philcade its name. The entrances invite foot traffic. The second floor too was arcaded but has since been converted into office space. St. Genevieve marble was used in the arcades, and extended to the ornamental plaster frieze at the ceiling. The ceilings were originally decorated with hand-painted ornamental plaster. Later the hand-painting was covered over with gold leaf.

The interior of the Philcade is surprisingly lavish, particularly for a building that was to be modestly designed. The arcades are distinguished by fluted marble pilasters that continue in an arch over the ceiling. The overwhelming perspective at the entrance is one of repeated stage sets, dazzling in the use of shiny metals and gold leaf. The gold-leafed opulence is further highlighted by beautiful, rich pastel colors. Hanging in the archways are elaborate filagreed light fixtures made by Empire Chandelier.

Fears about saturating Tulsa with an overabundance of office space were needless. R. N. Lattner, building manager, announced shortly after the opening that office space in the Philcade was 80 per cent occupied, and that he expected all the space to be taken in a short time. Oil companies accounted for a large portion of the rentals.

The shop space was quickly filled. Shops on the first floor included a cigar store, newsstand, barbershop, drug store, interior decorating shop, India import shop, and various ladies' clothing shops. The arcaded second floor was largely occupied by financial firms, including real estate brokers, investment, banking and mortgage loan companies.

In 1930 the officials of Standard Oil of Indiana were in Tulsa for the International Petroleum Exposition. Impressed with the city's growth and prospects, they decided to make Tulsa their Southwest headquarters. To do so, they would need to expand their office space in the Philcade. Negotiations began for an addition to the Philcade, and by the end of 1930, it was announced that new construction was to begin immediately, less than a year after the building's original completion. Four floors were added to bring the Philcade to its present thirteen-story height. While the foundation had allowed only for a three-story addition, an extra floor was gained by the use of lighter, haydite concrete.

Response to the Philcade's expansion announcement was enthusiastic and overly optimistic. It was heralded by the *Tulsa World* as "Lifting the few remaining Depression clouds that lingered on the Tulsa business horizon."[8] Indeed things were looking better. In early 1931 construction on the $1,500,000 Post Office was about to begin. Paving, sewer, and library contracts for $2,500,000 were out for bids, and the Union Depot was being rushed to completion at a cost of $3,500,000.

In 1937, with Leon Senter as architect, some alterations were made to the Philcade. The south side of the H-shaped building was enclosed to provide room for an air conditioning system. It was designed to supply chilled water to the Philtower as well as to air condition the Philcade. A fabulous streamlined penthouse apartment was also added at this time.

Two other buildings illustrative of the 20's Zigzag style lie beyond the downtown area. Both are low structures, of one and two stories. Built sometime between 1928 and 1930, Milday's Cleaners on 11th Street (old Highway 66) is a box-like structure that would have little to recommend it were it not for the lavish use of terra cotta.

Milady's Cleaners was owned and operated by Garabett S. Aghajan, an Armenian from Beirut, Lebanon, and his wife, Bertha. In addition to providing cleaning and dyeing services, Milady's had facilities for cold fur storage. The building contained special air-cooled vaults, and there was an underground fresh water spring utilized in the cleaning process.

A two-story building, the first floor is buff colored terra cotta, faced with variously sized ashlar blocks. The second floor is cream colored stucco to blend with the terra cotta. On the front and the one exposed side of this corner building are tall, wide windows, arched at the top, containing vertical panels of blue glass which are similar to the late English Gothic blue transom windows at the Gillette-Tyrrell Building. Surrounding the windows is sculptured terra cotta (now painted black and gold) which includes a potpourri of flowers, grape clusters, pears, pineapples, swans, and leaping stags. A band of floral terra cotta runs across the top of the first floor.

The second building, the Warehouse Market, may be better known to Tulsa historians for its location. It stands on the site of McNulty Baseball Park. Babe Ruth and the New York Yankees played there, as did Red Grange. Jack Dempsey fought there. McNulty Baseball Park also provided shelter for black families during the 1921 race riot when the Greenwood area was burned.

The Warehouse Market, sometimes known as "The Farmers' Market," sometimes just as "The Market," was built in 1929. John J. Harden, an Oklahoma City developer, negotiated a ninety-nine year lease with the McNulty family. Harden had started such a market two years before in Oklahoma City. Noting that the city's two main streets were constantly clogged with farmers bringing their produce into town, he decided to make use of some nearby underdeveloped property. He erected a public market to accomodate the farm sales.

Designed by Oklahoma City architect, B. Gaylord Noftsger, the Warehouse Market is a long, flat roofed, one story building, broken by evenly spaced pinnacles, and featuring a tall, stepped tower at the entrance. The building's

METALWORK AT ENTRANCE

TERRA COTTA WINDOW DETAIL

TOWER

only verticality is the soaring tower. It was a traditional Farmers' Market with open stalls on the east end near the viaduct that connected the Market to the old Midland Valley Railroad tracks. The tower portion acted as a landmark and a beacon to make the market dramatic and modern.

The Warehouse Market exhibits some of the most flamboyant examples of brilliant polychrome terra cotta ornament in Tulsa. The entrance is a close plagiarism of the famous entrance of the "Skyscraper in Rainbow Hues" (The Commercial Building, 10 West Elm, Chicago), later portrayed in catalogue form by Northwestern Terra Cotta Company of Chicago. This entrance for the Commercial Building was designed by the French modeler, Eduard Chassaing for Chicago architect, B. Leo Steif. Chassaing reduced nature to its basic geometric forms. Flowers and leaves became flattened circles and triangles, while the lines and patterns within these evolved into rays or chevrons.

The terra cotta at the entrance of Warehouse Market features Rococo-like neo-classical figures contained in medallions along with a variety of geometric designs in bright blues, greens, reds, and golds. The terra cotta ornamentation extends up to the top of the parapet and up to the top of the tower. The parapet is banded in raspberry, blue, and white terra cotta motifs including fans, rosettes, arcs, and rays. The tall, narrow tower is adorned with blue, white, and red diamonds in diagonally criss-crossing designs surmounted by a vine motif.

Two large medallions on a bright blue background flank each side of the entrance. One portrays a fecund goddess holding a sheaf of wheat and a cornucopia; the other depicts a god wearing a winged helmet, an oil derrick in one hand and a train engine in the other. The machine, speed, and transportation theme symbolized by the god is a precursor of the 30's.

The Market was the main supplier of Tulsa's groceries in the early 30's. It also provided artistic displays of produce, flowers, and table decorations. There was a butcher's department with fine cuts of meat, as well as a barber shop and beauty shop, restaurant and snack bar. Shoppers were entertained by live bands playing country music.

The Warehouse Market's popularity and prosperity were short-lived because of the Depression. Since that time it has had a varied history. It became the Club Lido in the mid-30's, featuring such entertainers as Benny Goodman, Duke Ellington, and Cab Calloway. The economy really could not support this kind of entertainment,

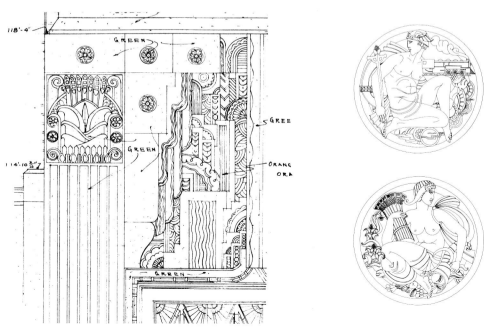

DRAWINGS OF ENTRY DETAILS

ORIGINAL GOTHIC STRUCTURE WITH FOUR-STORY ART DECO ADDITION

and in 1938 it once again became a grocery store. At the end of the 50's it became a liquor store, one of the first established when Oklahoma finally gave up prohibition.

The story of the 20's, with its move from the traditional to the rejection of the traditional is told in one building, the Southwestern Bell Main Dial Building. The original two-story building was built in 1924 in the conservative Gothic style. It was designed to allow a future addition of seven stories, and an addition was needed by 1930. Four stories were added to the building in the Art Deco Style, which by then had become widely accepted.

How thoroughly the Art Deco Style had become established is indicated by the comments of a Bell Telephone Company official: "Southwestern Bell is a conservative company, operated by conservative men. Naturally, their buildings reflect this. Since in the early 20's Gothic architecture was 'mainstream', that was what was built. By the time of the 1930 addition, however, Art Deco was a well-established commercial style."[9]

The attitude of Southwestern Bell Telephone Company toward the Zigzag Art Deco style architecture was but one indication of its overall acceptance. The ultimate endorsement came from the city government itself in the Skyscraper Style buildings proposed for the new civic center in 1930.

Although the growth of the city through the 20's was positive and exciting, for the city planners there were some growing pains. No one ever doubted Tulsa's eventual destiny as a major city. How best to ensure it was another matter. The City Plan Commission together with the Regional Plan Commission decided to seek advice from the well-known professional in the field, Harland Bartholomew of Bartholomew and Associates in St. Louis. Bartholomew was hired to study six different areas affecting the quality and direction of Tulsa's growth: major streets, railroad transportation, the revision of zoning ordinances, a civic center, public transit, and parks and recreation.

In studying the need for a civic center, Bartholomew determined that, for its size and projected growth, the city lacked an adequate Convention Hall, Court House, Municipal Building, Library, and Museum. In fact, Tulsa had no museum at all at that time. Bartholomew suggested a combination Art Museum and Indian Memorial.

Bartholomew examined eight possible locations for the civic center on the basis of certain criteria governing

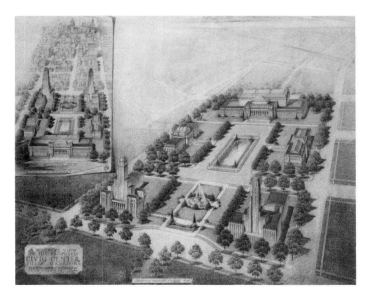

1930 PROPOSED CIVIC CENTER
LOOKING WEST FROM ELWOOD AVENUE

the selection of the site. The criteria were: a central location; an agreeable traffic pattern, with major streets bordering but not dividing the area; a location compatible with the trend of growth, neither creating a barrier to the normal path of business development, nor causing it to detour in an unnatural direction; a focal point for the city; a suitable neighborhood ideally located in a dormant area; an adaptable site; and finally the consideration of cost.

In considering the adaptability of the site, Bartholomew pointed out that one of the reasons that Tulsa's business district was so impressive when seen from a distance was that it lay on a knoll. The topography, area, and shape of the land involved should be borne in mind in the placing of the civic center.

The site that was recommended in light of the above factors was a 16.5 acre area lying between 3rd and 5th Streets and Elwood (incorrectly referred to as "Elmwood") and Houston Avenues. The principal feature of the civic center was to be the Municipal Auditorium farthest from the business district and facing toward it. In front of the auditorium and extending to Elwood Avenue an open plaza was planned, surrounded on three sides by the four remaining buildings, the combined Art Museum and Indian Memorial, the Library, and at the opposite end from the auditorium, the City Hall and the Court House. The City Hall and Court House were proposed as Skyscraper Style buildings, with set backs and tower terminations, reminiscent of Rockefeller Plaza.

The plan was never executed, probably due to the onset of the Depression. Tulsa historians speculate that the majority of the populace just was not quite ready for such a grand scheme. Furthermore, the Tulsa taxpayers alone would have had to bear the total cost since federal monies were not then available for matching funds.

Tulsa did not build its Civic Center until 1964. But thirty-five years after the Bartholomew study, the Civic Center was located only two blocks from the originally proposed site, an indication of Bartholomew's acumen.

*"A doctor can bury his mistakes,
but an architect can only
advise his client to plant vines."*

— Frank Lloyd Wright

In the 20's profits from oil built cathedrals, palatial residences, and major skyscrapers, and encouraged dreams of grand city planning. Overnight it would seem, Tulsa became a full-fledged city. The muddy streets, characteristic of an oil boom town, were paved. Muddy water ran clear with the development of the Spavinaw dam project. Two million dollars in bonds were voted for the schools. The Community Chest was established, the Federal Court constituted, and a new municipal jail completed and moved from the old livery stable section. Churches too were building and expanding to keep pace with the city's needs.

Given Tulsa's growth and building activity, it was not surprising that the city was able to attract architects of stature. Yet population growth was less important to the development of Tulsa's architecture than the statistics indicate. Statisticians are adept at manipulating data. The fact is that although Tulsa's population did almost double from 1920 to 1930, the doubling factor was not a figure in the range of 250,000. It was less than 72,000. By 1930, Tulsa had a population of just over 141,000 citizens. It was not New York; it was not Chicago. But Tulsa was building like New York or Chicago. It did not have the Rockefellers or the Wrigleys. It did have the Gettys, the Skellys, the Phillipses and the Sinclairs . . . a clientele for building monuments.

Three major architects with strong personalities, Francis Barry Byrne, Bruce Goff, and Frank Lloyd Wright, each built important structures in Tulsa during the last half of the 1920's. Byrne and Wright were imported for specific commissions. Goff lived in Tulsa until 1934, when the depressed economy compelled him to move to a larger city. His admiration of the Chicago architects drew him to Chicago.

Francis Barry Byrne (1883-1967), the Chicago Modernist, was brought to Tulsa in 1926 to design Christ the King Church. Christ the King began as Sacred Heart Parish when the Holy Family Parish in Tulsa was divided in 1917. A red brick church was completed and occupied in 1918, but the parish was expanding rapidly, and that church was quickly outgrown. In 1924 plans were begun for a new church to be built on a block of residential property purchased several years before.

Bishop Francis C. Kelley, the second Ordinary of Oklahoma was influential in the development of the new church. He had been the founder of the Catholic Church Extension Society, and was a prolific and published writer. He was also involved in the settlement of the sixty year dispute that culminated in a separate Vatican City in 1929. Beloved in Tulsa, a Tulsa high school is named for him. He was a dynamic man, experienced in fund raising and construction, and he intended for Christ the King to be a cathedral for the Tulsa Diocese.

Francis Barry Byrne of the Chicago architectural firm, Byrne and Ryan, was known to Bishop Kelley who had lived in Chicago. Byrne had designed several impressive churches, notably, Saint Thomas the Apostle in Chicago (1923) and Saint Patrick's Church in Racine, Wisconsin (1924). Through Bishop Kelley's influence, Byrne's firm was engaged to draw up the plans for the new Tulsa church. Bishop Kelley conceived and personally directed the project. He wanted Byrne "to make Christ the King something both modern and authentic to Catholic worship."[10] The church is "an expression of (Bishop Kelley) and (it) is proud that it was the first building of its style and that it predates Boston Avenue (Methodist Church)."[11]

Barry Byrne has been called the most imaginative designer of ecclesiastical buildings. He preferred working with brick, and students of Byrne have no trouble recognizing his style. Byrne was apprenticed to Frank Lloyd Wright from 1902 to 1907 and was one of the few older Prairie School architects who went abroad to study European architecture. His designs were affected by what he had seen. German and Danish influences are particularly noticeable in Christ the King.

The church itself became a very personal statement for both Barry Byrne and Bishop Kelley. It was their

SOUTH EXTERIOR

SANCTUARY

SAINT STEPHEN BY EDGAR MILLER

CASPAR BY ALFONSO IANNELLI

translation of a contemporary church. Christ the King Church is simple and straightforward. The design of the church, built around the Eucharist, was Byrne's attempt to see the church in a new kind of structure. Believing with Louis Sullivan that "form follows function," Byrne concluded that the church should function as an ediface existing to house the Eucharistic Altar and the purposes for which the Altar was erected. This was, in Byrne's own words, an "orthodox" conclusion.

There are few embellishments on the buff brick exterior except the finials of the vertical members which are reflected in the enrichment of the coping. The basic form of the building is a horizontal box, accented by tall vertical units. The interior detail is vertical, but the verticality is more apparent on the outside than it is on the inside.

The interior reflects a rich Gothic influence. The walls are of face brick adroitly executed in contrasting colors worked out in simple panelling with false quoins. The ceiling is of dark polished wood, sloping from a ridge at the center with slender beams from the ridge to the piercings where the windows occur.

The central space of the church, the sanctuary, is almost square, very unlike the traditionally narrow or cross-shaped form of the Catholic Church. The design of the space is related to the centrality of the Eucharist.

Since the church was built to be the cathedral for Tulsa as a separate diocese, the rectory for many years was used only by Bishops, and the church still contains the original Bishop's chair. This throne is a massive stone chair elevated above the sanctuary floor and recessed in a limestone trimmed niche with a limestone canopy.

The church evokes a feeling of tradition. It provides a fleeting glimpse of the Gothic. The materials used are very rich, more elegantly fine than elaborate. The sancturary lights designed by Barry Byrne and made by the Empire Chandelier Company resembled torches.

The carved limestone altar has deep horizontal flutings. A large mosaic of Christ the King, designed by Emil Frei, Inc. of St. Louis and made in Italy by the Ravenna Mosaic Company is empanelled behind and above the altar. Behind the two side altars at the front of the church are mosaics designed by Tulsa architect, Bruce Goff, and ordered through Frei and Ravenna.

Christ the King is a modern church but it was built by a community of artists with a philosophical concept of art work dating back to Renaissance times. The sculptor and designer, Alfonso Iannelli (1888-1965), worked closely with Barry Byrne on the design of the church. Byrne had met Iannelli in California through John Lloyd Wright. The architect and the sculptor had a very empathetic working relationship that is rarely found in this age. Iannelli made the statues of Saint Joseph and the Blessed Virgin in the side altars as well as the terra cotta ornament for the exterior of the church.

During the building of Christ the King a close friendship and future working relationship developed between Bruce Goff and Alfonso Iannelli. They would work together again in Tulsa, and then later in Chicago.

Byrne felt Iannelli's artistry was an important contribution to the spiritual feeling of the church. He said,

> "To give a feeling of aspiration suitable to the purpose, (plastic forms in brick enclosing the plan and structure) were made into vertical shafts with pinnacles of terra cotta. Terra cotta was selected for the ornamental parts because, being a clay material, it was closely related to the brick, therefore it unified with it. It also permitted a thing rarely done since the Renaissance, the actual reproduction of the sculptor's models in baked clay. Usually the architect makes a drawing of an ornament, a modeller (not an artist) reproduces it in clay, and the reproduction of that is then made and baked. The result is mechanical and lacks sensitivity. In this case, Mr. Iannelli, the sculptor, formed the actual designs into clay which were then baked, so that his artistic feeling, which is very great, was preserved in the finished product."[12]

The stained glass windows, executed by the Temple Art Glass Company of Chicago, were also done under the direction of Alfonso Iannelli. Edgar Miller's signature appears on one of the windows, and it is likely that he participated in their designs, for his "woodcut" influence can be clearly seen. Miller studied at the Art Institute in Chicago, and many of his stained glass panels, especially those designed for churches, originated in woodcut studies.

The windows on the south are the Kings of the Old Testament; on the north are the King-Saints of the Christian era. Four of the windows are signed: Saint Louis by Olive Rush, Saint Stephan by Edgar Miller, and Balthassar by Roger Miller. The remaining seven were apparently done by Iannelli, but only the one depicting Caspar is signed.

At the time of the church's completion, the architectural design and the stained glass windows were applauded by Maurice Lovonoux, the managing editor of *Liturgical Arts* magazine, and friend of Barry Byrne. He described the church itself as a "refreshing departure from the stereotyped structure," saying that the "buildings certainly fit into the American landscape." About the windows he wrote, "these windows rank among the best to be found in the United States . . . (they are) supurb in color and design."[13]

The church was completed in 1927 and dedicated by Bishop Kelley in May of 1928. It became the first church in the world to be dedicated under the name of Christ the King.

Marquette School, built in 1932, is the parochial school of Christ the King Parish. Significant only as it relates to Christ the King Church, it was intended to be an appendage to it. The school was designed by Frederick W. Redlich (1880-1950), to conform to the style that Barry Byrne created for Christ the King Church. To that end, it succeeds well.

Bruce Goff (1904-   ) started his architectural career the way many young architects did in the early 1900's. He simply went to work for Rush, Endacott and Rush, a Tulsa architectural firm. There was a major difference, however. Goff was only eleven years old when his father decided that the boy had wasted enough paper with his drawings of buildings. He summarily marched young Goff into the firm one afternoon after school.

William "A.W." Rush (1843-1923) and Arthur "E.A." Rush (1860-1948) were father and son whose architectural practice began in Grand Rapids, Michigan before the turn of the century. The Rushes moved to Chicago in 1910 and set up practice as A. W. & E. A. Rush. Their offices were in the Monadock Building, designed

TERRA COTTA SPIRES

ENTRANCE

by Burnham & Root and they were greatly influenced by the Chicago architects, particularly Burnham & Root, Louis Sullivan, and Henry Hobson Richardson.

Father and son came to Tulsa in 1912 as E. A. Rush & Company. A year later Asbury Endacott (1887-1944) joined them as a draftsman. He became a partner in 1915, and the firm was known as Rush, Endacott & Rush. In the same year the eleven year old Bruce Goff came to work for them after school.

The elder Rush started Goff on architectural exercises even though he was just a young boy. Goff's idolization of Frank Lloyd Wright began at about this time when he discovered books of architectural designs in the Rush, Endacott & Rush offices. He was doodling sketches that bore a striking resemblance to Wright's buildings before he knew who Wright was.

Goff continued to work for Rush, Endacott & Rush after school until he graduated from high school in 1922 and became a full-time draftsman for the firm. In 1929, on the completion of Boston Avenue Methodist Church, Bruce Goff was made a partner in the firm which was renamed Rush, Endacott & Goff. In 1930 E. A. Rush retired, and the firm became Endacott and Goff.

E. A. Rush was a "good, good architect who took care of the business."[14] Asbury Endacott, a fine structural engineer, also had some political aspirations. He was elected Water Commissioner in 1928, and was chief construction engineer in charge of the water and sewer plants at Mohawk Park. He ran unsuccessfully for Mayor of Tulsa in 1932.

Endacott was responsible for the structural drawings for the Boston Avenue Methodist Church, which included

WEST EXTERIOR

the structural calculations for the tower.[15] Endacott's son recalls that his father was up all night during the church's construction, working to remove the pillars from the downstairs community room.

To understand Bruce Goff's position at Rush, Endacott & Rush, it is necessary to understand the procedure for becoming an architect in Oklahoma before and after 1925. Until 1925, a builder or designer might simply declare himself an architect. There was no schooling, no testing, no licensing required. After 1925, architects in the State of Oklahoma had to be licensed. A "grandfather clause" automatically awarded a license to anyone who had been a practicing architect at the time. They simply registered and paid a fee. Everyone else wishing to practice architecture had to go to Oklahoma City to be tested by the Board of Examiners. Asbury Endacott was secretary-treasurer of the Board of Examiners in 1930.

Bruce Goff passed the licensing board examination to become a licensed architect on December 8, 1930. Until then he had been a draftsman and was considered the "star designer" for the Rush, Endacott & Rush firm. But it was not until 1930 that he could be called an "architect."

Reminiscing on his years as an architect, Goff frankly related that it used to bother him that his work could not be labeled a particular style, as could that of Louis Sullivan or Frank Lloyd Wright. Then he happened to read an article by a clothes designer in *Harper's Bazaar* magazine. The designer felt it was a mistake for a woman to be expected to wear clothes made for just anyone. She ought to wear the clothes that would bring out her own best features, characteristics, and beauty. This could not be accomplished by fashion's dictates. It needed to start with the individual. "Why wouldn't it be better to have something people could feel they were more a part of?" Goff thought. From then on he didn't worry about having a specific style. Each design had its own style.

Goff's first design project, a studio-house combination for his former art teacher, Adah Robinson, was a venture into the Art Deco style. Bruce Goff's acquaintance with Adah Robinson began at the time he was a student at Central High School where Adah Robinson taught art. "Goff was a favorite of Miss Robinson," according to Tulsa architect, Joseph Koberling, Jr., who was in the same class.

Adah M. Robinson attended the Chicago Art Institute and the West End School of Art in Provincetown, Massachusetts. She taught for four years at the Oklahoma City High School and for two years at the University of Oklahoma in Norman before accepting the teaching position at Central High School in Tulsa where she remained for nine years. Later she was head of the Art Department at the University of Tulsa from 1927 until 1945. She then moved to San Antonio, Texas where she became a professor at Trinity College.

Sometime in the early twenties "Miss Bobbie," as she was known to her friends, wanted to build her own house. It was logical that she would think of her "favorite student" Bruce Goff, whom she knew to work for an architectural firm. Goff remembers only that he had been out of high school for a fairly short length of time when Miss Robinson approached him about the design of her house. Preliminary designs were probably begun sometime around 1924, but because of Miss Robinson's limited finances, actual construction did not begin until 1926.

"Miss Bobbie's" house was designed to contain a studio and living space for a single woman. The house is massed in vertical rectangles, a design that would be turned on its side ten years later. This, however, being the age of soaring, the verticality was stressed by narrow proportions of projecting plan elements, heightened by chamfered corners. The house, inside and out, emphasizes simplicity, with white stucco walls and brown painted wood window trim. The only intricate patterning is in the leaded glass mullions of the two story living room windows. The angular shapes were repeated in the fireplace details, but these were later altered by Miss Robinson.

Goff worked with Adah Robinson on the design of her house, but lost interest in the project when the cost began to exceed her ability to pay. Joseph Koberling recalls that his father, who was a contractor and a mason, and a man named C. C. Hall, met together to figure out short cuts in order to get the house built. Koberling, Sr. did

NORTHWEST EXTERIOR

the masonry work, and young Koberling supervised the construction.

Koberling remembers an incident during the construction of the house. Mrs. Robert Boyce McArthur, a friend of Adah Robinson's, stopped by one day, poked around, and wondered where the kitchen was. There was a kitchen unit, albeit of the two burner variety, at the end of the dining room. Mrs. McArthur left and returned in short order with "Miss Bobbie" in tow. Miss Bobbie was visibly upset. "Mrs. McArthur says I have no kitchen," she told Koberling. "Oh, yes, you do. You and Bruce worked out a kitchenette unit at one end of the dining room. There it is on the plans," reassured Koberling. "Oh, dear, but we must have a real kitchen." In an all night design effort Koberling managed to work a real kitchen into the north corner of the house without disturbing the rest of the plan.

The Tulsa Building was a joint project of The Tulsa Club and the Tulsa Chamber of Commerce. The movement to build a headquarters for the Tulsa Chamber of Commerce and other allied business organizations began in the early 20's. During 1922, while the Chamber was raising $60,000 in building subscriptions, the men who would form The Tulsa Club were gathering informally in the offices of Rush Greenslade. By the next year this group decided to expand their meetings to include lunch, and they leased the basement of the Kennedy Building for that purpose. In November, 1923, they incorporated, and Rush Greenslade became the first president. Less than a year later the club had grown to such proportions that the membership needed a permanent location.

At that same time the Chamber was moving ahead on its plans to construct a building. They had a 99 year lease on their lot, and excavation had begun.[16] At this point, pursuant to the suggestion of A. L. Farmer, president of the Chamber of Commerce, The Tulsa Club began negotiations with the Chamber to combine efforts and to build the building together.

The Tulsa Club and the Chamber of Commerce formed the Tulsa Building Corporation and shared the cost of the Tulsa Building on a 60-40 per cent basis; The Tulsa Club paying the larger percentage.

The new eleven story building was completed on December 26, 1927. Rush, Endacott & Rush were the architects, and Bruce Goff was the designer. Built of Bedford stone, the exterior of the building has been described

ORIGINAL CLUB ROOM

DETAIL AT ROOFLINE

ORIGINAL 5TH STREET ENTRANCE

as a "simple rectangular building (with) linear piers which project in front of the window spandrels; the decorative termination of these piers is the one strong concession to tradition. At the original entrance, abstract geometrical detailing above the doorway and vertical light standards at the sides impart a Prairie School touch."[17] Sometime after 1951, a glass vitrolite band was added to the base of the building, vastly changing its appearance.

The Chamber, with other allied business organizations, occupied the first five floors, and The Tulsa Club occupied the upper six floors and roof garden. There was a central lobby 25 feet wide by 90 feet long, which served the dual purpose of clubroom and waiting room.

The Tulsa Club had dormitory rooms on the sixth floor, a gymnasium, turkish bath, and a barber shop. The barber shop had orchid vitrolite walls trimmed in a deeper shade of purple. On the eighth floor was the Men's Lounge, with panelled walls, big over-stuffed chairs and sofas, and a fireplace set off with mosaic tile. The original clubroom interiors had very geometrical Art Deco ornamentation that was repeated in column detailing, light fixtures, moldings and fireplace tiles.

Goff did some very original designs in glass for the building. There were peacock tails on the elevators and the chandeliers. The outside windows, however, posed real problems. They were made to open out, and when the wind caught them, they flew right off.

During the summer months, from June to September, the dinner service was transferred from the main dining room to an open air "roof garden." This was, of course, in the days before air conditioning. A beautiful tile terrace surrounded the building on three sides. Carrying the same theme as the main dining room but in modified form, the fixtures were strictly futuristic, including a panelled ceiling in pale green and orange. The building is now owned by The Tulsa Club which bought out the Chamber of Commerce in 1950.

Goff's next project for Rush, Endacott & Rush, was to design a warehouse storage building for Roy Page. Page chose the firm because it was one of the prominent architectural firms of the time and he wanted something different.

The project presented several interesting architectural problems. First, there was resistence to the commercial structure on the part of the residential neighborhood which adjoined the site. The warehouse location had been selected because of its proximity to the railroad tracks.

The second challenge from an architectural viewpoint was how to design a storage building for maximum storage space with the necessary structural supports. Goff's solutions to both problems were innovative and artistic. "The building has been called an example of honest architecture. Honest because it faithfully follows its purpose, plan, materials used, and methods of construction in its design . . . ."[18]

The initial study for the Page Warehouse showed broad horizontal bands graded from dark at the base to light at the cornice. Patterned like a modified ziggurat, each band was slightly recessed from the one below, further emphasizing the horizontal effect. Two vertical channels culminating in masts framed the central doorway creating a very distinct and formal entrance.

The final scheme which developed the theme of "continuous reveals" in brick, was less massive and expressed more directly the building's concrete flat slab construction. The entrance, which Page had requested be inviting, was of buff Bedford limestone and incorporated the "Page" name in a manner that was not only decorative, but was good advertising. The challenge of the neighborhood was met, because when the neighbors saw the building, they liked it. In fact, according to Roy Page, they were some of his best customers.

Flaring column capitals, or "mushroom columns," similar to Wright's Johnson Wax Building, solved the storage space versus support dilemma. These columns eliminated the need for intermediate beams by shortening the spans. The outer edge of the floor slabs and the perimeter columns were exposed to view, producing not only a decorative effect but also emphasizing the structural features. This emphasis on structure gave the appearance of great strength which was particularly appropriate to the building's purpose. The wire cut pinkish-buff brick was set in and hung on the frame with no attempt made to hide that it was the frame that held the brick. The effect of the weight was thus put honestly where it belonged, on the frame, and not on the lower brickwork.

The five-story building contained a basement with a cold storage room for furs. Special storage facilities also included a silver vault and a large rug vault. Pianos were stored on the ground floor and the rest of the building was devoted to furniture storage. A large elevator at the rear of the building could be loaded directly from the dock lying along the railroad track. The building was modern both inside and out; even the lighting fixtures were modernistically angular, of bronze and glass.

The Page Warehouse was demolished in 1977 and Page, now Page Van Lines, moved into another Goff building. Originally designed for Guaranty Laundry in 1928, Goff remembers it as "a low cost building." The building is a commercial one and makes no attempt to be otherwise. Again, the Goff emphasis is on the customer's entrance, and again, the building is organized horizontally. Horizontal bands are formed by projecting sills and lintels. The entrance becomes a focal point by interrupting the patterning. The doorway is further set off by diagonal mullions and bands of diamonds which accent the whole entryway by extending to the top strip of windows. A streamlined cornice appeared on the original plans in abrupt contrast to the sharp street corner it bordered. However, the streamlining of the corner was lost during construction.

Another Goff commercial warehouse was built in 1929 for the Midwest Equitable Meter Company. An eastern firm, with branch offices in New York, Chicago, Los Angeles, and other major cities across the country, the company chose Tulsa as a location "to meter the progress of the great oil industry."[19]

A presentation drawing, angular and geometric with an exaggerated upswept parapet, was overruled by the central office. Although the local manager of the warehouse liked the first scheme, it was rejected as not fitting into the composite photograph of the regional offices portrayed on the firm's calendar.

The original parapet was subdued, angled lintels and sills were straightened, and this revised design

ORIGINAL ENTRANCE

NORTHWEST EXTERIOR

ORIGINAL 11TH STREET ENTRANCE

was accepted. The building has corbeled brickwork, the tan bricks laid vertically, in soldier courses. The sides of the building are of glass block. According to the same article in the *Tulsa Spirit,* the building "embodied the modernistic motif." The 1929 building was in many ways a forerunner of a building style that would become popular in the 30's.

Combination studio-residences were a challenge that Goff particularly enjoyed, because they gave him an opportunity to provide design solutions tailor-made to the individual client. Here, as in no other circumstance, his penchant for personalized design could be allowed free rein.

The Riverside Studio was designed for Patti Adams Shriner, a musician and teacher who maintained eight studios in the city of Tulsa. Mrs. Shriner received her musical training in the United States and Europe, and was a scholarship pupil of the world-renowned Maurice Moszkowski. The building was to be used as her residence and combination studio and recital hall for her music students. It is similar to the Robinson studio in both plan and materials. There is a formal front entrance and double height lobby that provides access to the teaching studios as well as to the central recital hall. The high-ceilinged lobby is reminiscent of the living room-studio in the Robinson house. The stage acts as the link between the studio and residence. The kitchen and dining facilities double for residential use and studio functions.

Dominating the front elevation and facing the river is an enormous round window, patterned with sandblasted designs. On each side of the window, smaller rectangular studio windows are connected by black glass inserts to form diagonal patterns across the facade. Some have suggested that the windows look like the black notes on a piano keyboard.

Bedrooms on the upper levels open to roof terraces, a preview of the 30's terraces. The volumetric groupings and their relation to the hillside behind might have been influenced by the Frank Lloyd Wright precept that the

ORIGINAL SOUTHWEST EXTERIOR

ORIGINAL ENTRANCE WITH FOUNTAIN BY ALFONSO IANNELLI

ORIGINAL SOUTH EXTERIOR

FLOOR PLAN

"PIANO MUSIC"
3' x 12'

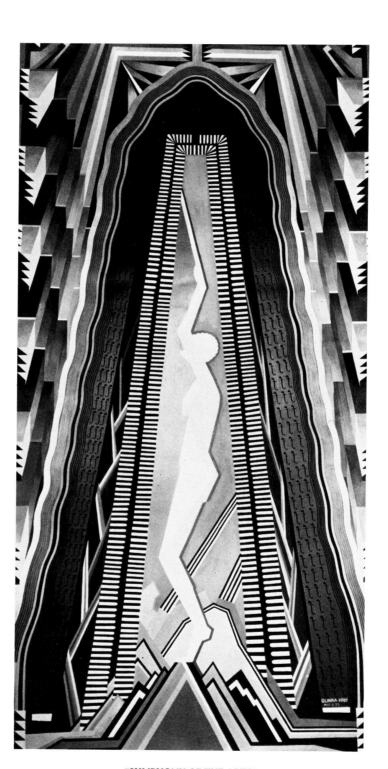

"SYMPHONY OF THE ARTS"
9' x 16'

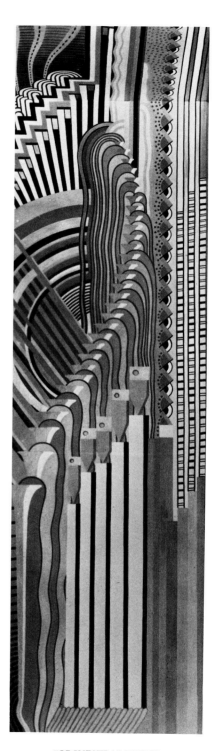

"ORCHESTRAL MUSIC"
3' x 12'

structure be a part of its site: "No house should ever be on any hill or on anything. It should be of the hill, belonging to it, so hill and house could live together each the happier for the other."[20]

The residential wing originally included walls papered with light green Japanese wood veneer, aluminum ceilings, and fireplaces of black glass and green marble. The interior walls of the recital hall were once lined with murals representing the different forms of music.

Olinka Hrdy, a talented artist, part Czechoslovakian and part American Indian, painted the series of nine murals. These murals were among the first adventures in abstract decoration in Tulsa. Goff had suggested the murals for the interior and had also recommended Olinka Hrdy.

Two talented ladies, each a prima donna in her craft; the results were predictable. Patti Adams Shriner hated the colors as they went on the walls, although she had approved of the same colors earlier. She complained to Goff; he tried to lessen the tension. Finally, the two women confronted one another—ostensibly over the color scheme. Patti Adams Shriner accused Olinka Hrdy of ruining her studio. She elaborated by saying that the green on the walls was the color of jealousy and envy; the red, passion and hate . . . . Exasperated, Olinka interrupted, fixing Mrs. Shriner with an icy stare. "There is only one color you should use," she announced. "What color is that?" asked Mrs. Shriner somewhat curiously. "White!" declared Olinka, triumphantly. "White is the color of insanity!" Each retired to her respective corner, and Goff, who had introduced artist to artist, was left to intercede so that the project could be completed.

Olinka Hrdy had the last laugh. Patti Adams Shriner had been most adamant about not including any musical reference to jazz, which she considered an abomination. One of Olinka's murals, innocently abstract, was made up of small triangles of different colors that spelled out "JAZZ." Apparently, the intruding word did not show up in color, but did when it was photographed in black and white.

Alfonso Iannelli designed a fountain for the studio, which was the centerpiece of the entrance steps. It was made of black, orange, and white terrazzo with chromium metal. The fountain that remains is no longer recognizable as the original work.

Mrs. Shriner was forced to give up her studio in 1933. The building now houses the Spotlight Theatre, known for its Saturday night performances of "The Drunkard."

Tulsa was an Indian trading post of 500 people when the Methodist Church was chartered in 1893. The church became known as the "Boston Avenue Methodist Episcopal Church South" in 1907 when it built a three-story structure at the corner of 5th Street and Boston Avenue. The church's membership kept pace with Tulsa's growth, and by 1922, when Dr. John A. Rice was appointed pastor, he found that Sunday School classes were being held in the Y.W.C.A., a public school, and the Orpheum Theatre. It became Dr. Rice's task to build a new church, the fourth, for the growing congregation.

A building committee was appointed in 1925, headed by C. C. Cole. Five architects submitted designs (the firm of Rush, Endacott & Rush was not among them), but none was what the committee wanted. Mrs. Cole suggested that they might seek the advice of her good friend, Adah Robinson. Supervisor of art at the Tulsa Central High School, she was also the supervising art teacher for the church's educational program and Director of the Tulsa Art Association.

Adah Robinson met with the building committee, listened to their ideas for a church, and felt that she could translate them into a tangible building if she were allowed to work directly with an architect of her own choosing. Her choice was her former student, and the architect for her own house, Bruce Goff.

"Goff relates that he prepared sketches . . . Miss Robinson . . . then presented them to the building committee. The preliminary designs proved acceptable, and a contract was signed with Rush, Endacott & Rush on

June 26, 1926 . . . ."[21] Adah Robinson was given a contract by the church stipulating that she was to be supervisor of "all matters artistic, both in interior finish and outside design."[22]

This working arrangment forms the basis for a controversy that continues in Tulsa even today, more than fifty years after the completion of the church. It centers around the role played by Adah M. Robinson and the attribution of the design credit for the church. It is not the purpose of this book to offer a resolution to that controversy.[23]

"The completed building changed remarkably little from the first conceptual sketches. In plan, a semi-circular auditorium is joined to a linear wing of classrooms and supporting facilities by a wide hallway developed as a 'Social Lobby.' This lobby connects two lateral entrances which are articulated by towers. A third entrance on axis with the altar leads through the educational wing to a porte cochere for arrival by automobile."[24] The porte cochere was a new concept, a beginning recognition of the role the automobile was to play in the future. Before renovation in the 60's, there was a roof garden over the porte cochere that was used for summer meetings and concerts.

Although resembling the work of Louis Sullivan and of Barry Byrne's Christ the King Church, the plan of the church was also developed in response to the particular siting. Situated on a plot of ground at the intersection of three streets, the church was designed to be viewed from any angle. There is no rear to the church. The most imposing facade was intended to be a focal point on Boston Avenue for approaching traffic from downtown. In recent years Boston Avenue has been made a one-way street, with traffic moving away from the church toward downtown. Now without a hurried glance in a rear view mirror, that perspective, at least from the automobile, is lost.

On Boston Avenue, Boston Avenue Church's 255 foot tower is the central and dominant feature. At the first set back of the tower is a chime loft sheathed in copper and ending in a steel and glass finial of four fins, designed to reflect light in dramatic patterns.

The building is surfaced with Bedford limestone ashlar blocks and buff-colored terra cotta spandrels. Goff described the building as an example of modern Gothic. The aspiring line, repeated in pointed arches, and culminating in the soaring tower, certainly recalls Gothic tradition.

The church's greatest significance as a completely modern concept lies in its expression of spiritual ideas and the symbolism of those ideas that is carried throughout. Adah Robinson, a Quaker, immersed herself in the study of Methodism for an entire summer. In *A Twentieth Century Church*, Robinson wrote:

> "The concept of a modern church should reflect the ideas, ideals, and philosophy of our modern Christianity. The plan of the Boston Avenue Methodist Church South is an attempt to express the highest aspirations of Christianity, to make evident in form and color the power of spiritual thought, to release the tension of the human mind to a nobler freedom of imagination, as in music, and to assure the hurried passer-by of the reality of the Infinite . . . . Modern religion is vital and of continuous growth; therefore the place of worship should not be final, ominous, conscious of wealth or temporal power, but by a vertical dominance of line suggest the open mind. Closed lines and horizontal lines have been associated with finality. Modern lines are upward, open and free. Hence the designs of the finials, the praying hands. The closed, clasped hands of the Middle Ages signify the intensity and fear of the supplicant. These modern hands, open, are confident of the receptivity of Divine Grace."[25]

The open, praying hands were much noted and discussed by critics of the new church. They found the design "new and startling," and they liked it.

The theme of Robert Garrison's terra cotta sculptures on the exterior of the church revolves around the historical events of the Methodist church. The figures include John, Charles and Susanna Wesley and Frances Asbury. Also portrayed are the circuit riders, so much a part of religious history in the West. Garrison had been a pupil of Adah Robinson's in Oklahoma City.[26]

The motif for the windows and one that is carried throughout the church's decoration is derived from two flowers indigenous to Oklahoma, the tritoma and the coreopsis. The flaming red of the tritoma signifies the exciting nature of the Christian faith, and the profusion of petals, its generosity. The deep-rooted coreopsis, thriving despite adverse circumstances affirms the harshness of the Western frontier. It symbolizes the strength of the Christian love for the Church and its members. The tritoma can be found repeated as a decorative design in the panelling, the plaster cornices, the wood carvings, and bordering the terrazzo floors.

In the sanctuary the stained glass windows are inset in a V-shaped plan, creating a play of lights. Beveled glass is used extensively, adding a dimensional quality as well as a vibrancy and sparkle to the windows. The tower windows are of a tapestry glass that was sandblasted and set in copper.

The semi-circular sanctuary, with its domed ceiling, light filtering from the top and sides, gives the impression of a huge, open bubble, a favorite 20's form. From the height of the dome, 80 feet in the air, the ceiling slopes gently, ornamented in plaster with a very modern and very simple design.

The chapel is quietly subtle with repeating religious symbols lending an atmosphere of reverence. Crosses occur in the panels between the windows. The windows themselves are conventional, stained glass, and designed for meditation and peace. The ceiling is bordered by a frieze with carved processional figures.

The colors used throughout the church were termed "atmospheric"; that is, there was to be no direct consciousness of any one hue. All colors were to be suitable to every room and to provide the maximum light.

Renovations in the 1960's by McCune and McCune, Architects, included work on the sanctuary and the addition of a new educational wing. When the addition was completed Boston Avenue Methodist Church became the second largest cantilevered building in the United States. The church was built for an original investment of close to $1,500,000.

The building achieved worldwide recognition for its innovative use of modern architecture in expressing contemporary Christianity. It is included in the *Encyclopedia Britannica,* as is Christ the King Church, as an example of a 20th century church. Boston Avenue Methodist Church is honored on the wall of Chicago's Tribune Building

• • • • • • •

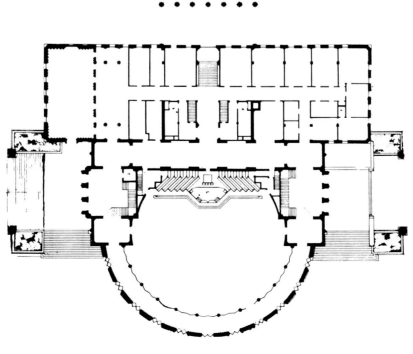

FLOOR PLAN

SOUTHWEST EXTERIOR

as one of the architecturally significant buildings in the world.

Alfonso Iannelli, sculptor and artist for Christ the King Church, wrote of Boston Avenue Methodist Church: "Here is a church that is religious and aspiring, lofty, inviting too, with a completeness and resonance that is entirely in accord, full of hope and youth . . . Here is a building that is a voice of the 20th Century, giving joy to beholders!"[27]

Sheldon Cheney, one of the most respected architectural critics of the time, wrote in his *New World Architecture:* "But it is in Tulsa, Oklahoma, that the most provocative American example of different church building has emerged. The Boston Avenue Methodist-Episcopal Church is a form that anyone would recognize as 'church-like' at a distance or close-by, inside or out. Its style begins with the accenting of the aspiring line. But its detail is daringly new, its ornamental idioms fresh and vital, its masses fairly well sculptured and perfectly expressive of plan."[28]

The modernistic Christ the King Church must have been a tremendous source of inspiration to Goff. There were only a handful of Art Deco churches across the country (probably fewer than a half a dozen) and Goff had one in his own back yard. Furthermore, Goff was very familiar with Christ the King having designed the mosaics in the side altars.

Certain details, such as the angular doorway frames, and the finials of the sanctuary walls, recall comparable elements by Byrne in Christ the King. The pleated effect of the tower and sanctuary windows seem more aligned with contemporary examples in Europe, and Goff himself attributes his awareness of the work of the German Expressionists to conversations he had with Iannelli and Byrne in 1926 and 1927 when all met during the construction of Christ the King.

CIRCUIT RIDERS

EXTERIOR LANTERNS

SEMI-CIRCULAR SANCTUARY

GREAT HALL (SOCIAL LOBBY)

TRITOMA MOTIF IN GRILLE

TRITOMA MOTIF IN PLASTER MOLDING

STAIR RAIL DETAIL

TRITOMA MOTIF IN CHOIR STALL

TRITOMA MOTIF IN TERRAZZO FLOOR

SANCTUARY STAINED GLASS

ROSE CHAPEL STAINED GLASS

Although the churches are quite different, they are also quite similar. Both are vertical in detailing. Both sanctuaries, although different in shape, are huge centralized spaces. The architecture of both churches could be labeled "American Expressionistic." They carried on a European tradition of expressionism, developing it into the popular Art Deco. They are modern buildings with the capacity to evoke a sense of tradition.

The Merchants Exhibit Building (1930) was a new structure that was built beneath the existing grandstand of the fairgrounds. The grandstand seats were the demarcation point, the building having to conform to the circumscribed space. The grandstand was 685 feet long and 100 feet wide, and bore the distinction of being the longest building of its kind west of the Mississippi River.

The superstructure for the two-story building was of brick, concrete and steel. The unusual brickwork in alternating layers of dark and light tan was outlined in stone trim. According to an article written about the building when it was new, Tulsa brickmen and builders had never seen this variation of brickwork. The main entrance was dramatically steeped in a Mayan corbeled pattern, the entire building giving the effect of a "striking modernistic design."

Ornamental metal work and the specially designed light fixtures were made of stainless steel. Lights were recessed into niches between each of the thirty-eight panels that made up the modernistic exterior. Lights were also built into the stone work above the main entrance and the six supplemental entrances, and turquoise blue glass was used to create a dramatic effect.

The first floor of the building provided space for the exhibits, booths, wide aisles, and a spacious lobby. The second floor was devoted to quarters for the exhibitors, dormitories, showers, and space for a later cafeteria.

The Exhibit Building is no longer in existence. It was built near a coal mine, where mining activities had allegedly been confined to an area far removed from the site. But the building was lost when half of it settled into the mine.

Bruce Goff is credited with "honest architecture." This is particularly evident in the commercial structures he built in the 20's; precursors of things to come. His commercial buildings were horizontal masses, the style of the 30's, but he could not give up the verticality at the entrance. He compromised on occasion, by using diagonals. The look was geometric.

For the commercial structures, the warehouses and the laundries, the surfaces were simplified. Instead of

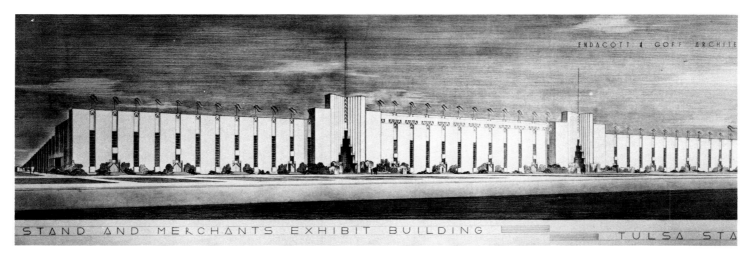

EXTERIOR ELEVATION

using applied ornamentation, the building material itself created decorative interest. The pattern and color of the brickwork, served as ornament.

The buildings whose form was intended to be aspiring, (Boston Avenue Methodist Church and The Tulsa Club Building) were vertically organized buildings. The studio-residences were still massed on a vertical axis. Frank Lloyd Wright would organize "Westhope" on the same planes. But there was beginning to be a subtle change. The late 20's were not quite so soaring.

Bruce Goff had met his idol, Frank Lloyd Wright, on a trip to Chicago to inspect terra cotta samples during the construction of the Boston Avenue Methodist Church. He went with his friend Alfonso Iannelli on a day's trip to Taliesin, where he met Wright for the first time. In 1929, Wright came to Tulsa to build the Richard Lloyd Jones house.

"Westhope" (1929-1930) was more than a fusion of building blocks; it was also a fusion, and on occasion, fission, of two dominant personalities — the client and his architect. The client, Richard Lloyd Jones, was founder and publisher of the *Tulsa Tribune.* The architect was Frank Lloyd Wright, his first cousin.

"It was a flint-and-steel proposition," wrote Richard's son, Jenkin Lloyd Jones, present publisher of the *Tribune,* "for they played together and fought each other as children, and they carried on a love-hate relationship for nearly nine decades."[29]

Jenkin Lloyd Jones suggests that his father may have resented Wright's greater eminence, because Jones loved to tell disparaging stories about Wright's extravagance. One of Jones's favorites was about the time he was a young magazine editor in New York in the early 1900's. Wright, stranded in New York with no money, came to him for a loan so that he could get back to Chicago. Jones "coughed up the money" and an hour later Wright was back, this time with something rolled up under his arm. It was a beautiful Japanese print, and he still needed money to get to Chicago.

But Jones remembers that his father admired his cousin too, and when he decided to build his own house, he wanted Wright to design it. This was in the late 20's when Wright often went for months without a commission. His cousin still, in a manner of speaking, was lending him the money to get to Chicago.

Construction got underway after about eighteen months of discussion. The preliminary sketch had been for a rambling house of wood and stucco, Japanese style, with a low-pitched roof and surrounding courtyard. Wright

1930 AERIAL VIEW

changed his mind about the design after visiting the site. Instead, he advised a 90 degree angle house, composed of a series of vertical pillars of dry-tamped concrete.

The concrete blocks were molded on the premises. They were a unique feature, Mayan in patterning, and used inside and out in the house's construction. They serve such diverse functions as outside walls and inside space dividers. They conceal heating and lighting equipment.

Vertically stacked windows, forming columns of clear glass, are contained between the pillars. The window dimensions, matching those of the blocks, form a transparent screen that threads its way into the fabric of the house.

"Westhope is fundamentally spatial because of its generous, open floor plan, modulated with shallow broad steps and changes of height."[30] The ceiling is lowest at the main entrance. Opposite are four steps down to the dining room. "This step by step opening up of the interior tends to pull one into the form; the attraction is unmistakably calculated." The feeling is one of a theater entrance — the floor drops and the ceiling becomes higher. It is awesome.

An enclosure of the three levels of the house, appearing like a tower, was an afterthought according to the late Mrs. Richard Lloyd Jones. "There was no purpose to it at all. Richard and Frank agreed! And one day there it was, a disruption of the otherwise low silhouette. Our house was meant to be close to the ground in the fashion of the Japanese, not a dominant feature of the landscape."[31]

The original pitched roof was abandoned in favor of a flat, tarred roof, covered with paving stones. This was an untried Frank Lloyd Wright innovation. At this time in his career Wright could not afford testing laboratories, so he simply tested as he built. Unfortunately this first roof was one of his experimental failures. According to Jones:

> "The roof proved little better than a sieve. The paving stones were removed and the roofers called back. It still leaked. During one cloudburst, while the family was dashing about the living room with buckets and pans trying to save the rugs, my mother stood in the middle of the disaster and said with an acid Irish wit, 'Well, this is what we get for leaving a work of art out in the rain!' On another occasion my father furiously got on the long distance phone to the architect. 'Dammit, Frank,' he roared, 'it's leaking on my desk!'
> The calm voice from Wisconsin replied, 'Richard, why don't you move your desk?'"[32]

MOLDED CONCRETE BLOCKS

ENTRANCE

EAST EXTERIOR

PENCIL RENDERING BY FRANK LLOYD WRIGHT

PENCIL RENDERING BY FRANK LLOYD WRIGHT

By the time the house was under construction it was the beginning of the Depression, and both men's finances had become strained. The original plan had been to have the whole house, including the carpets, reflect Wright's craftsmanship. But because of the cost, these details were omitted. Even so, Wright was eminently satisfied with the results. He said at a banquet held in the large dining room, "The damned thing's more beautiful than I ever expected!"[33]

"Westhope" was both a beginning and an end for Wright. It represented the beginning of his Usonian period in that it was "a dwelling place that has no feeling for the 'grand' except as the house extends itself in the flat parallel to the ground—a comparison to the horizon."[34] And indeed, rising from the prairie, as it was originally built, without landscaping or human reference, it is a house without any sense of scale. The Usonian house of the succeeding decades included "the cubiform cluster, with its tail of rooms, the glass bay, and clerestory cluster arrangement" all of which originated here.[35] Westhope was also a terminus for several Wright designs that belong to the Art Deco. Included in these are "the chevron-cross pattern, the perforated mask, the enclosed glass bay, and the pier screen." The strong sense of Art Deco in Westhope is not dependent upon ornament. It is in the vertical emphasis of the pier screen that creates the image of the Skyscraper Style.

After Richard Lloyd Jones's death, Mrs. Jones sold the house to M. Murray McCune, of the architectural firm McCune & McCune. His restoration of Westhope included the installation of central air conditioning. McCune had grilles made from the original lighting molds so that the new air outlets would be of the same motif. The kitchen was expanded and the patio enclosed. An architect who appreciated the Wright design, McCune went to great lengths to preserve the spirit of Westhope as Wright had built it.

To some Tulsans Westhope has been dubbed "the pickle factory," a nickname that originated with Richard Lloyd Jones himself. One weekend he went to visit the site of the house under construction. The huge building, rising as mysteriously as Stonehenge, had attracted a number of curious sightseeers. "Puzzled onlookers . . . wanted to know what was being built. 'A pickle factory,' Jones replied. 'Do they HAVE to build them like this?' they asked."[36]

During the 20's many of the old conventions were discarded, temporarily at least, in favor of anything new and modern. Attitudes were ripe for the lavish, carefree new architectural forms of the Zigzag Art Deco. The style was a mirror image of a time when sophistication was the vogue, and blasé the byword. Cole Porter wrote "Anything Goes," and it did.

In 1929 the bubble burst.

▼
▼

P W A

"Never was a country
in the throes of more capital letters than the old USA,
but still we haven't sent out the SOS."

— Will Rogers

By the early 1930's the popular nonsense song of the decade before, "Yes, We Have No Bananas!" had become prophetic. An architect summed it up this way: "Ten years were just erased from my life—at a time when I had all that energy and a young family. There was no work. There was *nothing*."[1]

The Depression was insidious and undefinable. It was emotional; a loss of faith; finally a panic. It is hard to pinpoint the moment that Tulsa felt is effects. There was a lag across the country from the October, 1929 stock market crash to the unequivocal onset of the Depression. But by the winter of 1931 its repercussions were felt across the nation and soup lines formed in Tulsa. Despite Waite Phillips's addition to the Philcade, despite the pending opening of the Union Depot in the spring, despite the construction of the Municipal Airport Administration building and the Post Office, and despite the enlargement of the Federal Building, people were out of work, and they were hungry.

Beggars came daily to the doors of the more affluent asking for money for food. Often the same sad, hollow-eyed children appeared with different sets of "parents." Most people were proud and carried on as if nothing had changed but of course there were changes.

A Tulsa real estate broker explained that Tulsa was more fortunate than many cities, and it certainly was in terms of the wealth that supported its architectural ambitions. The Texaco and Mid-Continent refineries continued to operate. The Sand Springs industrial community, just across the Arkansas River, was viable, and the Sand Springs' employees spent their money in Tulsa. Downtown Tulsa was really the only place to shop. Most of the oil men had their money in oil, not the stock market and their investments protected Tulsa's downtown. The Chamber of Commerce was strong, and had monied members.

Although oil prices dropped drastically, the oil men continued to make money during the Depression. People on salaries had their wages cut, but were grateful to have a job. Employers instituted what might facetiously be termed a "spread the poverty plan." By 1933, for example, Tulsa's City and County governments were forced to lay off workers, and in order to keep layoffs to a minimum, instituted a rotating "Payless Weeks" program wherein employees did not get paid for some weeks of work. Everybody owed everybody money and they paid when they could.

In response to the national situation, Franklin Delano Roosevelt provided a "New Deal" for the country, with its own set of monogrammed initials. Much of the New Deal legislation is an integral part of our lives today; the SEC (Security and Exchange Commission), FHA (Federal Housing Authority), and FDIC (Federal Deposit Insurance Corporation), are familiar governmental agencies. The New Deal also left us many governmental buildings unique in their architectural style.

Construction was stimulated under the auspices of two New Deal agencies, the Public Works Administration (PWA) and the later Works Progress Administration (WPA). International Stripped Classicism, a style of architecture that has humorously been referred to as "PWA" was beginning to emerge in major projects even before the enactment of the PWA programs. Although PWA and WPA did not decree design, certain labor and material restrictions that were inherent in the programs resulted in some fairly uniform practices. Generally, these buildings were massive, bulky, and ornamental.

The Public Works Administration was founded in 1933 to increase employment and purchasing power through the construction of useful public works. The PWA planned or approved plans and supervised its own projects. The ultimate control was in Washington. PWA programs did not hit their stride until the business recession of 1937-38, because it took time to detail specific plans for large projects.

The Works Progress Administration (WPA) was created in 1935 to provide a variety of public works projects for the large numbers not employed by the construction works. The agency undertook to supply jobs for anyone who needed them. It provided work for skilled as well as unskilled laborers. It set up projects for writers, musicians, actors and artists. It has been estimated that 80 per cent of the nation's top-ranking artists were on the WPA rolls at one time or another.

The PWA Art Deco is a transitional architecture. It incorporates elements of the Zigzag Art Deco of the 20's and the Streamline Art Deco of the 30's. Most of the buildings in this style are characterized by their monumentality. They are largely governmental buildings or buildings funded in part by governmental agencies. Their size and bulk convey an image of strength, solidity and permanence, a sign of reassurance to a disillusioned nation.

The classical use of symmetry in this architecture reflects the Zigzag 20's. The principal entrance to the building is emphasized and there is an occasional suggestion of an entablature and cornice. The use of ornament in relief sculpture, murals and mosaics is traditional. The ornament often illustrates the building's function. Symbols of nature and of the machine are combined and the common laborer is often glorified in the ornamentation. Man is usually shown nude, his bulging muscles symbolic of strength and power.

The PWA style was more severe than the earlier Zigzag style and the ornamentation and building material relied less on the use of color. Horizontal features were adopted from the International Style and the occasional use of curved corners suggested the Streamline. Windows were often placed together to give the impression of a horizontal band. The buildings are an interesting combination of the Zigzag and the horizontal emphasis of the Streamline. An example of this architectural style is the massive Tulsa Union Depot.

Until the opening of the Union Depot in 1931, Tulsa had a haphazard arrangement with the three main railroad lines that serviced the city. Each line, the Katy, the Santa Fe, and the Frisco had maintained its own separate station. For years there had been efforts to unite all of the services.

A number of plans had been proposed and rejected by both the city and the railroads. The grade of the rail tracks into town was the major stumbling block. The tracks and yards were so near the level of the Arkansas River bridge that they could not be lowered much further. Therefore it was necessary to raise the streets in order to eliminate downtown grade crossings.

The first step toward the eventual construction of Tulsa's Depot was taken on December 6, 1927, when voters approved a bond issue of $1,250,000 to finance a share of the cost of grade separations and the resulting property damage. With that money earmarked, in 1928 the railroads and the city settled on the following plan. Main Street was to be elevated over the Frisco tracks, while Boston Avenue, which had been closed for years, and Cincinnati Avenue were turned into viaducts.

The station was originally planned to be three or four stories in height and was to cost more than a million

NORTHWEST EXTERIOR AND COVERED CONCOURSES CIRCA 1932

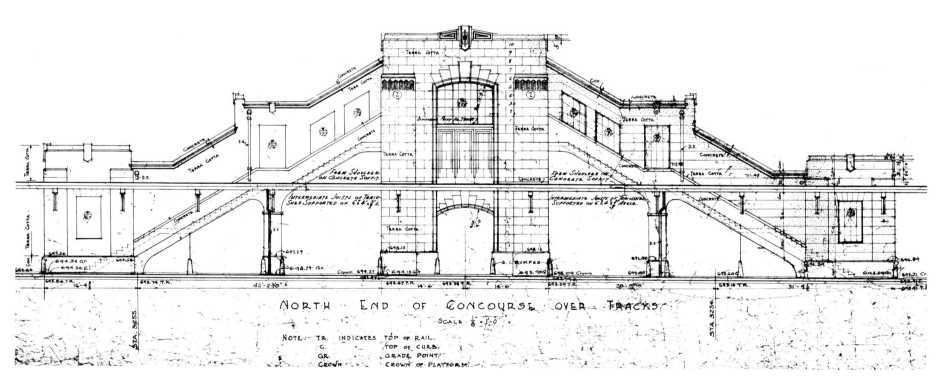

NORTH END OF CONCOURSE OVER TRACKS

WAITING ROOM

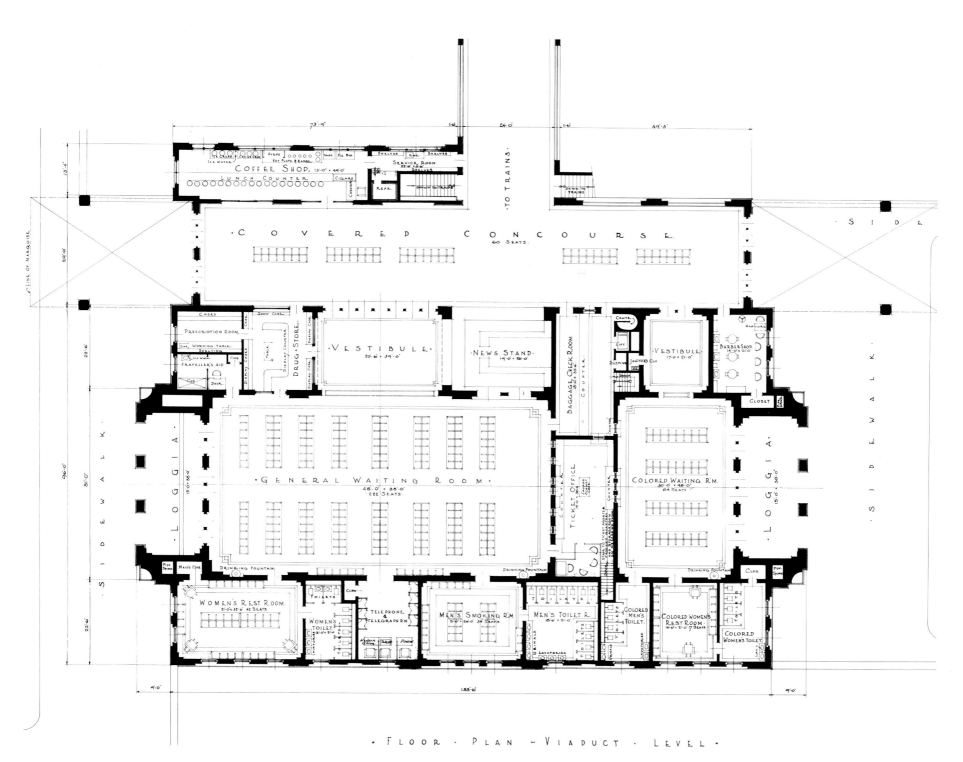

· F L O O R · P L A N ~ V I A D U C T · L E V E L ·

FLOOR PLAN – VIADUCT LEVEL

dollars. The building that was eventually built comprised just two floors and a mezzanine. There was a track or ground level service floor and a main floor at the viaduct level. These floors were separated by the mezzanine which provided facilities for Red Caps and "colored train porters." The depot was to be built on the site of the old Frisco station but on the south side of the tracks. Boston Avenue was no longer obstructed.

The city bore half the cost of the street improvement through the bond issue, and the railroads serving the city paid the other half and built the depot for a cost of $3,500,000. Ground was broken for the Union Station Depot in November, 1929. Tulsa labor was used exclusively in its construction and the Depot was completed in less than two years.

An elaborate grand opening was held on May 12, 1931. The Union Depot was heralded as Tulsa's most magnificent improvement in recent years and called Tulsa's "most important front door." The completion of the depot was viewed by many as a turning point in the economy signifying the end to the Depression. Opening day included a parade, a banquet, marching bands, dancing on platforms, and the resurrection of "Old 94," the famous Frisco locomotive that pioneered the line into Tulsa. The entire program was broadcast by KVOO radio, the Voice of Oklahoma. It was estimated that between 50,000 and 60,000 people visited the terminal during the opening day. They came from as far away as California. Officials from the Frisco, Katy, and Santa Fe Railroads were on hand.

The monumental Union Depot, its stripped classicism, massing, and its impressive bulk, is an example of the PWA Moderne. A Frisco Railroad official wrote at the time the building was designed; "In formulating the scheme it was the aim of the designer to emphasize the functions of the building with a . . . frank expression of a modern problem, making no attempt to follow any traditional or historic style . . . ."[2] Designed by R. C. Stephens, chief architect for the Frisco Railroad, the exterior walls are faced with variegated Bedford stone. The effect of a cornice is achieved by a carved Greek key motif, broken by conventional shield designs which bear modernistic figures of eagles and winged wheels in bas-relief. Other ornamentation includes motifs inspired by Central and

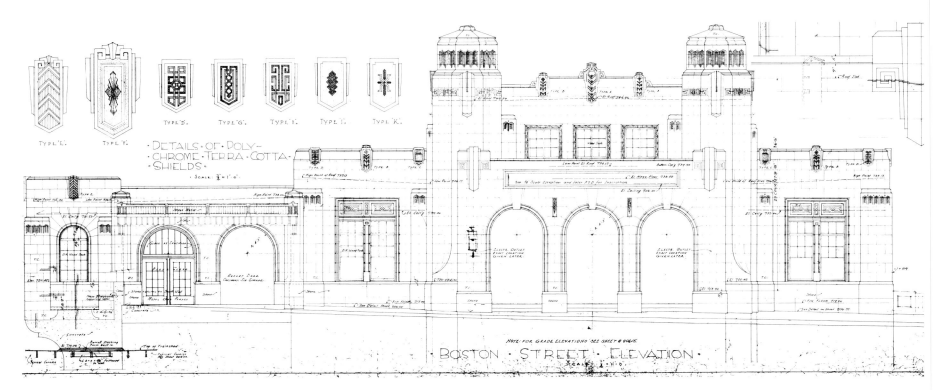

BOSTON AVENUE ELEVATION

North American Indian art.

The depot extends almost a full block from Boston Avenue to Cincinnati Avenue. It is 300 feet long from north to south, including the covered concourse over the railroad tracks. The total interior space, including the terrazzo floored concourse, is 27,000 square feet.

The entrances to the Depot were segregated. The black's entrance was to the east; the white's to the west. Both entrances had octagonal towers astride a triple arch. An elaborate marquise, with copper sheeting and glass drops hanging like curtains, covered the entrances.

The waiting rooms were on the main level. They were two-story (35 foot ceilings in the white's waiting room, 32 foot in the black's waiting room) with clerestory windows at the top for light. The waiting room walls were made from marble and travertine and the floor was marble inlaid with terrazzo. The ceiling and borders were tinted in pastel tones. The directional signs, "To Trains," "Ladies," etc. were vermillion colored neon letters, electrically lighted in statuary bronze frames. Two large clocks, synchronized with the other clocks in the station, were set into the walls above the east and west doors. The segregated black and white waiting rooms, entrances, and restrooms were separated by the ticket windows, the baggage room, and the telegraph counter on the main level. A travelers' aid room, newsstand, barber shop, coffee shop, and drug store, were also located on the main level.

The baggage handling facility was geared to the faster paced travel. A spiral steel chute sent the hand baggage from the station to a checkroom at mile-a-minute speed. The lower level at the end of the chute was a service area. It contained baggage storage, the hand baggage room, dog kennels, the mail room, the station master's office, rooms for porters, and supply closets.

During the Union Depot's short-lived heyday as many as thirty-six passenger trains serviced Tulsa daily. The popularity of train travel was at its acme when the Depot was completed. But after World War II its dominance began to be eclipsed by the growing airline traffic.

On May 12, 1967, just 36 years after its proud opening, the lights of the Tulsa Union Depot were turned off and its doors locked. Now it stands, a behemoth of another age.

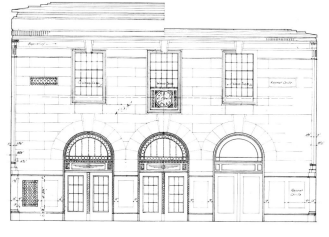

ELEVATION LOOKING TOWARDS EXIT

INTERIOR ELEVATION

TERRA COTTA AT EAST ENTRANCE

ROOFLINE TERRA COTTA

CORNER DETAIL

Less than a year after the Union Depot opening, 7,500 people attended another opening. The Tulsa State Fairground Pavilion, the city's first large auditorium, was built for the Charity Horse Show. The building was the largest in the Southwest, with a seating capacity of 10,000, including the 100 by 200 foot arena. The total floor space covers ten and one half acres. Built with no interior columns, the roof is supported by a truss that creates a dome, an unusual structure for the 1930's according to Ray Jordan, Tulsa County Engineer. Leland I. Shumway, architect for the Bliss Hotel, designed the Fairground Pavilion and its "nationally recognized floating roof."[3]

The Pavilion, built at a cost of $275,000, is a blond brick building with colorful terra cotta ornamentation. Projecting panels break the building's facade, creating a linear look. The windows are contained between these projections which terminate above the roofline as pinnacles of terra cotta. There are eight entrances; four large entrances centered on the north, south, east, and west sides of the building and four smaller arched entrances cutting the corners and forming an octagon.

Panels of multi-colored terra cotta flowers in low modeled relief provide a background for the heads of a horse,

EXTERIOR CIRCA 1949

a steer, and a ram. These animal heads repeat and form a horizontal band around the roofline of the building. Each entrance is set off by decorative terra cotta. The large panels over the main entrances show livestock and men against a background of palm trees. Terra cotta panels of horse's heads are located above the arched entrances. The use of terra cotta in this building is unusual and is its most interesting feature.

Another of Tulsa's PWA Art Deco buildings which is unusual and elaborate in its use of terra cotta is the Tulsa Fire Alarm Building. The building was the center of an alarm system which was one of the two major municipal improvements necessary in 1930-31 for the city to obtain a lower fire insurance class rate. To be approved by the National Board of Fire Underwriters, the station had to be located at a minimum distance of 150 feet from any other structure. The clearance requirement was to protect the building from fire in an adjacent building. Thus, the Central Park site was selected.

The cost of the building and of the total alarm system, was paid for by a bond issue. Built to house the centralized electronic equipment for receiving and dispatching alarms, the building contained thousands of cables

NORTH EXTERIOR

GARGOYLES AT ROOFLINE

TERRA COTTA FRIEZE

TERRA COTTA PANEL AT ENTRANCE

LANTERN WITH ETCHED GLASS

and wires run underground. These carried signals from red "Gamewell" alarm boxes located throughout the city. When the white handle of the alarm box was pulled, the signal was transmitted to the Fire Alarm Building where dispatchers noted the location and signalled the closest fire station. All communication was effected via "Gamewell" tape, which was similar to ticker tape.

The Fire Alarm Building was designed by Frederick Vance Kershner while he was employed by Smith & Senter. Kershner was one of the young architects who took advantage of the opportunity to learn from different people and in 1930 he left Arthur M. Atkinson's office to go to work for Smith & Senter.

Leon Senter, architect of the Philcade, was regarded as the dean of Oklahoma architects. When the licensing law went into effect in 1925, he was issued License #1. He was president of the State Board of Governors of Licensed Architects in Oklahoma and a charter member and past president of the Oklahoma Chapter of the American Institute of Architects. Senter was the architect of several PWA style buildings in Tulsa.

Kershner quickly learned that Senter liked decoration and "fuss." Senter's constant injunction to his employees was, "Make it gay but not gaudy, boys!" Kershner, whose Beaux Arts background was undoubtedly to his advantage, became adept at this.

The buff terra cotta ornament on the Fire Alarm Building was inspired by Kershner's Mayan temple design which had received an award from the Beaux Arts Institute of Design in New York City. The elaborate terra cotta panel above the front door of the Fire Alarm Building is of an Adonis-type male, stripped to the waist, with Gamewell alarm tape running through his hands. Flanking him from behind are two helmeted firefighters. Winding through the composition are stylized hoses, the nozzles appearing as fire-breathing dragons. Lightning bolts radiating from the central figure suggest speed and energy.

On either side of the central panel are small terra cotta plaques of Gamewell alarm boxes. Around the outer course of the building are fire-breathing dragons. Gargoyle heads decorate the back. Small panels ring the building with dragons, firefighting axes, and nozzles.

Built of blond brick and heralded as Tulsa's most fire-proof building, the doors, the window sashes, and all of the furnishings and trim of the interior are metal. The roof is gypsum. The basement housing the auxiliary power system was excavated by manpower in an attempt to spread employment. The light fixtures in the front of the building have been jokingly referred to as "Classic Mussollini Official Lanterns." They are characteristic of the PWA style in their massiveness.

The Tulsa Municipal Airport Administration Building (1932) was also designed by Frederick Vance Kershner for Smith & Senter. A three-story building of steel and cream colored stucco with rounded Streamline corners and Zigzag decorations, it contained elements of the vertical style of the 20's and the horizontal style of the 30's.

A circular drive in front of the building allowed cars to drive under the decorated metal marquee. The corresponding arrangement on the plane side of the terminal had been planned to allow the largest transport planes to taxi through with motors running, but it was never actually used that way.

A three story square observation tower was set back from the front entrance of the building and flush with the rear, or plane side. The roof of the tower was octagonal, clad with metal, and topped by an electric beacon. Rounded Zigzag pillars at the corners of the tower contained terra cotta panels of stylized two-blade propellers. In the top floor of the tower was the control room enclosed by window walls. Below it were the offices of the weather bureau, and below those, the offices of the airport manager.

The terminal also provided a restaurant and kitchen, men's and women's lounges, and a large high ceilinged waiting room with a terrazzo floor. It housed offices of the Department of Commerce, Post Office, and the air lines, including United, Bowen, Braniff, Transcontinental, and Western. Two additional wings were part of the original design for the terminal, but were not financially feasible and were never built.

Elaborate terra cotta ornamentation symbolizing flight illustrated the function of the building. This decoration was applied extensively to the exterior and interior of the building. Kershner worked with Northwestern Terra Cotta of Chicago on the detailing of the design. A bird-in-flight motif in terra cotta was used above the four decorated bronze and glass doors on either side of the terminal. A course of decorative terra cotta with birds circumscribed the building above the first floor windows. The terra cotta panel over the front entrance featured a monumental, helmeted, winged figure, of indeterminant gender, but probably female. "She" was geometric, with large wings sweeping up and out creating the impression that they radiated from "her." At the top was a bird (probably an eagle) swooping down with wings extended to land on a sphere representing the globe. Two tall sections of heavily floral terra cotta flanked the figure, completing the panel.

The decorative bird motif was extended to the inside as well. A plaster panel located above the exit door was the focus of the interior decoration. The theme of the panel was transportation through the ages. The newest and most up-to-date tri-motor plane was the central feature, its two-blade propeller set at a jaunty angle across the nose, and its narrowing wings thrust out at each side. Beneath these wings the older forms of transportation were represented in profile: an automobile, a locomotive, a horse, and a man on foot. A profusion of fluffy clouds filled the air. Above the cockpit of the plane a circular space enclosed a clock.

The Tulsa Airport actually had come into being in 1928 as a result of a crash program for Tulsa to be a part of

PROPOSED TULSA AIR TERMINAL
ADMINISTRATION BUILDING
DESIGNED IN 1928 BY JESSE L. BOWLING AND
ISADORE SHANK OF ST. LOUIS, MISSOURI

The most unusual features of this "modernistic" design were the 20' high doors at either end through which planes could pass with motors running to load and unload passengers. The stucco building was designed to include waiting rooms, baggage rooms, ticket and business offices, lounges, a dining room and a roof garden with a dance floor where parties could be held.

INTERIOR

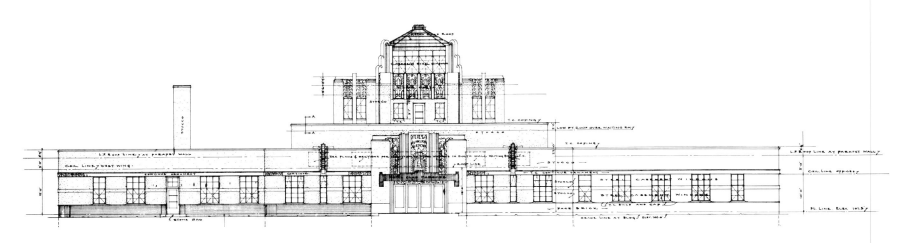

SOUTH ELEVATION

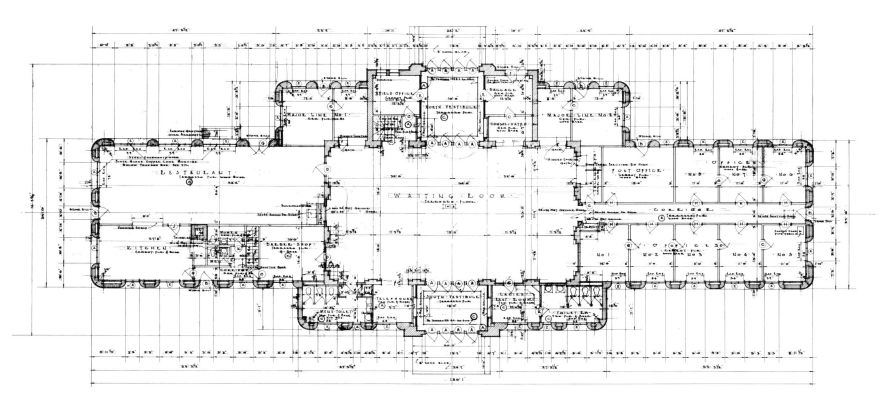

FLOOR PLAN

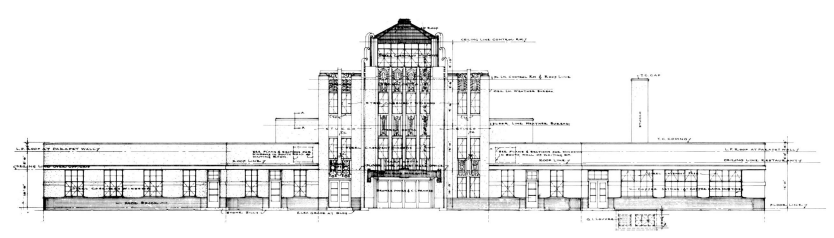

NORTH ELEVATION

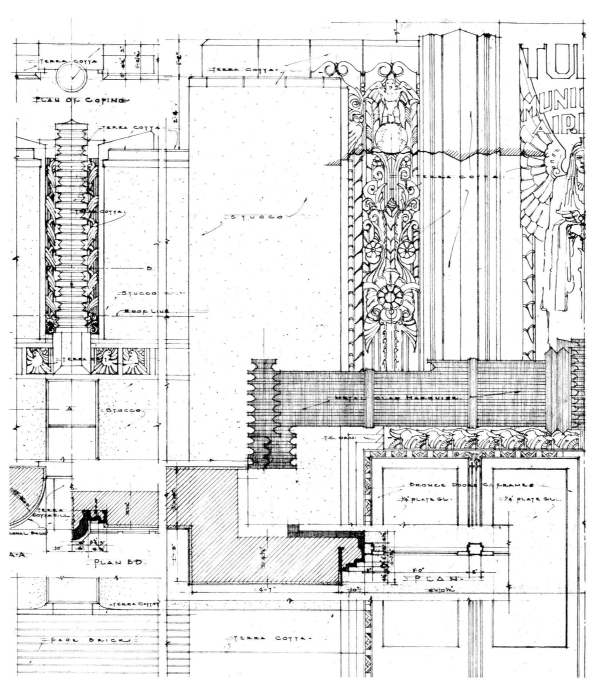

DETAIL OF STREET ENTRANCE

the Ford Reliability Tour. The airport, from location of site to erection of the first "administration building," went from dream to reality in six short months. The city and the Chamber of Commerce's enthusiasm for aviation, were behind this herculean achievement. A "stud-horse note" was signed on January 21, 1928, by forty-seven Tulsa businessmen and civic leaders to buy a 390-acre tract of land for an airport. The "stud-horse note" derived its name from a not uncommon farming practice. Farmers needing a new stud horse for their herds, would get together and go to the bank to sign a note for the purchase price, guaranteeing the amount and agreeing that any fees paid for the stud service would go to retire the note. Tulsans adopted this financing technique for several civic improvements. Mohawk Park owes its existence to the "stud-horse note."

On July 3, 1928 the Ford Reliability Tour came to Tulsa. The visitors found dirt runways carved out of wheat fields. A wind sock flew from the tar paper roof of the first administration building, a one-story frame shack painted Aviation Red. The airport was dedicated that afternoon and the first air mail left Tulsa in a Pitcairn biplane on July 6, 1928.

Operation of the port was carried on privately from July 3, 1928, to December 5, 1930, by The Tulsa Airport Corporation, whose members included Waite Phillips, William G. Skelly, Omer K. Benedict, Harry Tyrrell, Cyrus S. Avery, Harry Rogers, Robert Garland, and Charles W. Short, Jr., the manager. In 1929 the citizens of Tulsa voted $650,000 in airport bonds, and retired the "stud-horse note." Tulsa had an airport belonging to the city and within three years it had a new administration building.

An air show was the highlight of the opening day ceremonies for the new building on March 24, 1932. Celebrities attending included Wiley Post, Jimmy Doolittle, Art Gobel, and Frank Hawks. Aviation was developing at such a rapid rate that planning, no matter how far-sighted, could not keep pace. The terra cotta tri-motor plane depicting the newest form of air travel, was outdated by the time it was modeled. Similarly, the terminal, inadequate in size almost from the day it opened, was soon obsolete.

In 1934 Tulsa's downtown bus depot also proved inadequate to meet the city's needs. It was a temporary structure situated on a leased piece of land on the northeast corner of 4th Street and Cincinnati Avenue. Smith and Senter, Architects, were hired by Pickwick-Greyhound Bus Lines of Kansas City to draw up plans for a new depot. The site chosen was one block away from the temporary structure on land belonging to the Elks Club. The plans for a new structure included a seven-story hotel. The entire third floor was to be given over to the Elks in exchange for a ninety-nine year lease on the property. However, the deal fell through when the Elks vetoed the project.

Waite Phillips, impatient with the situation, stepped in. He purchased the land where the temporary station was located and undertook to build his own Union Bus Depot. He contacted the major bus lines, Pickwick-Greyhound, Southern Kansas Stagelines, and Missouri, Kansas and Oklahoma busline, to lease the depot to them for ten years with the stipulation that other lines be allowed to use it on a sub-lease basis. Phillips then engaged his friend and architect, Leon Senter, to design the building.

Construction began in September, 1934 and the Union Bus Depot opened its doors in February, 1935 with much fanfare. Public inspections, speeches, music and dancing, and a parade highlighted the event. The Depot operated on a lease basis until 1938 when Howard Allen of MK&O bought it from Waite Phillips.

The quality and the detailing of the structure were unusual, particularly for a public building privately financed in the Depression. Robert Allen of MK&O postulates that this is due to Waite Phillips's influence and ability to carry out such a project. Described by the contemporary press as "modernistic," the building is a potpourri of Zigzag and Streamline styles almost as if its design had been left to the flip of a coin.

The original building was two stories on the 4th Street side and a full three stories on the Cincinnati Avenue side. In 1950 the third floor was extended to make it a three-story building. According to Frederick Kershner who was the principal designer involved in the building of the Depot, one of the major problems was the size of the site. A partial solution was found in the use of a staggered marquee which extends over the loading platform and allows the servicing of six buses simultaneously.

      The exterior of the building is cream colored stucco and red brick. A black iron streamline canopy sweeps around the structure. Glazed ceramic tile, a Streamline favorite, sets off the two large windows of the coffee shop. The doors into the waiting room are framed by colored mosaic tile and glass brick. Six dock signs for the buses are in popular Streamline black glass with dock numbers and arrows in silver.

      A dominant feature of the Depot was the forty-seven foot high sign at the corner of the property. Its terra cotta base incorporated Zigzag motifs of chevrons and curves. The sign itself flashed "Bus Terminal" and "Union Bus Terminal" in red and green neon light.

      Black, orange and tan ceramic tile along with Egyptian styled chromium decorations adorn the interior of the Depot. The floors are gray, brown and black terrazzo. The original space provided for segregated waiting rooms.

EXTERIOR CIRCA 1935

There was a men's smoking lounge with shower and bath facilities, a coffee shop, ticket office, and newsstand on the first floor. The women's lounge and a conference room for bus officials occupied the mezzanine. The small third floor area was used for office space.

From the mezzanine one still can get a sense of the building's proportions. There are elongated octagonal windows above the two main doors on the mezzanine level. The walls are broken by fluted columns. An iron railing surrounds the mezzanine and continues down the stairs, its design carrying out the pattern of much of the interior. The building received national recognition as an example of modernistic design in a bus terminal.

If unskilled labor objected to the PWA programs as benefitting only construction workers, contractors felt that the WPA programs discriminated against them. They had qualified crews, but the government, under the WPA, was putting unskilled workers in their place and giving them job training. The WPA was equally frustrating for the architects, who had to act as their own general contractors in the detailing of their jobs, i.e., the breakdown of labors, materials, and hours. The PWA had allowed competitive bids for general contractors. Finally, to add insult to injury, the architects were not allowed to supervise the construction on WPA jobs, because the government had its own teaching supervisors who acted in that capacity.

A wide range of jobs fell under the purview of the WPA. The ideal that the agency set for itself was to provide the unemployed with the kind of work for which they were best suited. Unskilled labor found jobs on projects such as the construction of county roads and city streets, the improvement of parks, and the building of flood control. Skilled labor (carpenters and plumbers, etc.) was used to erect or repair schools, libraries, city halls, and other public buildings.

The criteria set for the selection of WPA projects were that they have public usefulness; that a high proportion of the funds used be spent on labor; that they not interfere with private employment; and that they be completed in one year.

Tulsa architect, Frederick Vance Kershner recalled the bureaucratic snarls involved in one WPA school project. He was hired to install eighteen toilets for the boys' and girls' bathrooms at the Schulter, Oklahoma school.

MEZZANINE RAILING

UNDERSIDE OF CANOPY

TERRA COTTA ROOF DETAIL

ROOF DETAIL

ROOF DETAIL

BASE OF SIGN

Since the government furnished the money, the job had to conform to WPA guidelines; one being that at least 90 per cent of the job's cost had to be in wages for labor; the other 10 per cent could be in materials.

Kershner used up his 10 per cent materials allowance just buying the eighteen toilets. He went to the head of the Oklahoma WPA with his problem.

"I've got two miles of pipe to lay, and those trenches have to be filled in with crushed rock. I've used up my materials allowance with those eighteen fixtures for the bathrooms. What are we going to use for crushed rock?"

"Any stone around the place?," he was asked.

"Yes ---"

"Then hire lots of laborers to crush stone."[4]

The Schulter WPA project became known as the job of the many stone masons, one indication of why Oklahomans claimed that WPA stood for "We Piddle Around!"

In all the WPA-PWA controversy, one point is not disputed. Had it not been for these programs, a lot of small communities would never have had the facilities they have today. Before 1939 ended, PWA had sponsored projects in all but three counties within the U.S. at an estimated cost of nearly six billion dollars. In many instances, and certainly in Tulsa, PWA bore only part of the expense of a project; the rest was borne by a local taxing agency. WPA was even more far-reaching. By 1941 it had employed eight million individuals or about one fifth of all the workers in the country. In six years it spent over eleven billion dollars.

Of the WPA-PWA programs in Oklahoma, architect Joseph Koberling said, "We built so many schools that we were called the 'great educators' for a while." The first PWA projects in the state were two Tulsa High Schools: Will Rogers and Daniel Webster. Will Rogers High School, the more traditional of the two, is typical of the PWA Art Deco.

SOUTHWEST EXTERIOR

ENTRANCE

LANTERN AT ENTRANCE

The selection of architects was left to the School Board. A. M. Atkinson was the supervising architect for the Board, but he had no voice in the selection of the other architects. His function was to give a brief description of the projects, and then to act as go-between for the School Board and the architects. The architects for Will Rogers High School were Joseph R. Koberling, Jr. and Leon B. Senter. Koberling said of the school: "We emerged from classicism . . . to express our own times."

Funding for the school was obtained from the school district, which paid 55 per cent and from the PWA, which paid 45 per cent. The school was designed to accommodate 1,500 students in a spacious setting. School planners were sent from Kansas City to design the floor plan. There are 200,000 square feet (five acres) of floor space and almost twenty-seven acres of grounds. The site was chosen because of the number of feeder schools and the projected population growth. The school had a multi-level gym, but the tennis courts have given way to additional parking space.

Will Rogers High School was designed to inspire pride and to instill school spirit. It is an elaborate school building. Two terra cotta plaques over the front door give a pictoral history of Will Rogers's life. One panel portrays the earlier period—Will, smiling his famous smile, in the pose of his monologue days; a horse, roped steer, and corral in the background. The other panel depicts his later interests—polo, movies, radio, and aviation. These plaques were researched and designed by Joseph Koberling and modeled by John Sand. A native of Luxembourg, Sand attended art schools in Europe and emigrated to the United States in 1920 to work as a sculptor and modeler for Northwestern Terra Cotta in Chicago.[5] The plaques were to appear in several Northwestern Terra Cotta company catalogues. Terra cotta plaques over the other set of front doors show a boy and a girl, each with books, a globe, and other symbols of learning.

Terra cotta spandrels containing vertical accents with dark and light shafts for contrasts also adorn the building. They were "just a design from the end of my pencil," said Koberling. The modeling on the spandrels was done by Karl Kolstad, a nephew of Kristian Schneider, the chief modeler for Louis H. Sullivan. Schneider was

CEILING FIXTURE IN FOYER OF AUDITORIUM

AUDITORIUM GRILLE

AUDITORIUM

STAGE

known for his masterful execution of Sullivan's intricate floral and leaf treatments. The spandrels were exhibited at the Merchandise Mart in Chicago in 1938.

The main hall of the school gives the impression of a fine office building with terra cotta sheathed walls and terrazzo floors. Materials included 9,892 pieces of terra cotta in the main corridor alone. Large arches at the doorways add to the sense of spaciousness. Ornamental plaster work borders the ceiling and was done by Percy Prosser, a well-known sculptor. Prosser would make a clay cast of a design that could then be repeated for hundreds of feet. Decorating the two main hallways were fifty giant sepia-toned prints depicting the seven phases of Roger's life from his early boyhood, through his motion picture career, to his role as the "ambassador of good will."

With "progressive" and "innovative" the watchwords of the day, results from recent studies about the psychology of color were incorporated into the interior color scheme. The original class rooms were all painted in pastels, color-keyed to learning. Colors were used to produce moods, correlating to the subject. Stimulating colors were employed for mathematics and science and quiet colors were used for the library. Five different colors made up the scheme which was later adopted by the whole school system.

The balconied auditorium resembles a luxury theater. The elaborate stage is curved and fluted with brass insets of a fan and floral design in tan, gold leaf, and terra cotta red. The proscenium is a dazzle of decorative floral designs, classic figures, fans and fountains in gold leaf, terra cotta red, and brass. Sumptuous brass lights and false balconies add to the theatrical atmosphere. The plaster ceiling is ornate, decorated with painted, cast plaster beams. Dominating the west wall of the auditorium is a mural painted by Alex Rindskopf, a Chicago interior decorator. The James Greenleaf Whittier verse about westward expansion is illustrated with figures of pioneers and Indians.

Construction began on the school on October 11, 1937. On September 11, 1939, the school opened its doors to 1,501 students. Dedication ceremonies were held during the week of November 3, 1939, to coincide with the sixtieth anniversary of Will Rogers's birth, November 4, 1879.

Tulsa's progressive PWA high schools were noteworthy enough to merit attention in a *Time* magazine article "outlin(ing) the high school pattern of the future."[6] A picture of Will Rogers High School was included and Tulsa was designated as "one of the most Progressive school systems in the study . . . ." The article continued, "Tulsa . . . built two model Progressive high schools, named one for Will Rogers . . . ." The other progressive school referred to, although not specifically named in the article, is Daniel Webster High School.

Daniel Webster High School is a precursor of schools built during the 40's. It has an enduring, fashionable neutrality that is much more modern than Will Rogers High School.

When funds first became available for the new school, the Board of Education decided to start naming high schools for presidents and chose "George Washington." Several decorative "W's" were incorporated into the design of the building. Residents of the area complained that the school would be confused with Booker T. Washington High School in North Tulsa, and asked that the name be changed. To make use of the "W's" the School Board selected the name "Daniel Webster."

The massing of the building was designed to complement the topography of the land. The front of the school is long and horizontal with two large wings angled forward. Massive, stepped rectangular columns flank the main entrance, setting off the school name and an enormous clock. Constructed of buff brick, the variety of patterning in the brick lends a modernistic design. Vertical buff brick piers contrast with spandrels of buff and burnt umber rowlock brick.

Three tiers of stairs divided by brick planters lead to the main entrance. Transom windows above the three entry doors contain a fan and volute silver ironwork design. Cast aluminum spandrels separate the entry doors

NORTH EXTERIOR

from the windows above. The Regency style influence, almost undefinable in the rest of the building, proclaims itself in the classic Greek motifs in each of the three panels. The central focus is an octagonal plaque containing a Greek column ringed by a laurel. The plaque to one side portrays a female figure; to the other side, a male figure, both with torches symbolically lighting the way of learning. A Greek fret pattern borders the top of the panels. Two huge silver metal torch lanterns in the PWA style are positioned at the front entrance. Smaller versions of these torches light other entrances.

The main auditorium repeats the fluting on columns above the marble wainscoting. The stage is new. Marble was removed to allow for a sound system, but the remaining ornamentation is original. Vertical designs bordering the stage include brass clocks and grillework with fret patterning. The light fixtures are original—three tiered squares of opaque glass with geometric metal stripping.

Although the exterior of Webster is unaltered, the interior has changed, due in part to the fact that the original materials were not so fine as those used at Will Rogers. The main halls have wainscoting of gold tile. The linoleum flooring has been replaced. The original library had a decorative ceiling, which has been covered over, and the area is now used as a classroom.

Three architects were selected by the School Board for the design of Daniel Webster High School. A. M. Atkinson served as supervising architect with William H. Wolaver (1900-   ), John Duncan Forsyth (1886-1963), and Raymond Kerr (1891-1943). The office of William H. Wolaver became the architectural home base for the planning of Webster High. Wolaver did the preliminary drawings, floor plans, specifications, and design. John Duncan Forsyth and Robert E. West (1904-   ), who worked for Forsyth, were responsible for the exterior elevations and the working drawings. Raymond Kerr participated in the drafting.

The School Board was responsible for providing a share of the funds with the PWA for the building of Webster High, and money was scarce. They ran out of money before the stadium was completed. A convoluted land and money exchange involving a simultaneous three-way switch was effected in order to raise the necessary funds.

William G. Skelly had pledged money to the University of Tulsa for a stadium, but he was forced to default

CAST ALUMINUM PLAQUES AT ENTRANCE

EXTERIOR LANTERN

because of the Depression. The University had a stadium, but was deeply in debt and needed quick cash. At the same time, the School Board needed a stadium for high school events and money to complete the athletic facility at Webster High. Waite Phillips acted as the catalyst. The Public Schools owned the land where Phillips's Philtower office building was located. Phillips wanted to own, rather than lease, this land. He bought the land from the School Board, giving the School Board enough money to complete the Webster High facility and to buy Skelly Stadium from the University of Tulsa, which the School Board then leased back to the University. The University got out of debt; the School Board got a stadium and construction money; Phillips got his land, and everyone benefitted. Later, the University of Tulsa was able to repurchase Skelly Stadium.

Daniel Webster High School came into being in 1938 to serve all of Tulsa west of the Arkansas River, an area of heavy industry and small businesses employing much of the blue collar population. Until the school was built, students from West Tulsa continued to cross the river to attend Central High School.

When Webster opened on November 6, 1938, it had an air-conditioned auditorium and individually heated classrooms. There were two gymnasiums, with a sun porch for sun treatments. Seven hundred sixty-seven students were enrolled. Dr. N. L. Engelhardt, Education Consultant of New York City, who assisted in the construction of over 300 schools, including Will Rogers, said of Webster High, "The architects grasped the vision of what the high school of the future should be like and planned Daniel Webster, building in cooperation with the entire educational staff of the Tulsa system."[7]

AUDITORIUM CEILING FIXTURE

AUDITORIUM FOYER

S T R E A M L I N E

1 *3* *6*

"Today, speed is the cry of our era . . . ."

— *Norman Bel Geddes*

While the economy was at a standstill, speed became the passion of the 30's. No one quite knew where he was going or what he would find when he got there, but it was important to get there quickly. Most chose to go by automobile. Will Rogers remarked that America was the first nation in the history of the world to go the poorhouse in an automobile. The automobile irrevocably changed American life. The impression one has when looking through photograph albums of the time is that young Americans posed for photographs with their new cars and sometimes remembered to include the new baby too.

Speed and the automobile permeated all phases of American life. A new kind of high-speed crime developed, requiring the "getaway car." The infamous gangs of bankrobbers, "Pretty Boy" Floyd and the much romanticized "Bonnie and Clyde," rampaged across Oklahoma in a modernized version of the stage coach robbery days. They careened through the towns in their automobiles cutting a swath of terror through the state. The banks, already hard-pressed by the Depression, found their insurance rates doubled.

Streamline was the rhythm of the 30's. Jazz was smoothed into swing, but the underlying current was swift. The need to get through the time propelled everyone forward. It was reflected in the horizontally streamlined architecture.

The depressed 30's built horizontally and simply. Everything went flat — the economy, the buildings, and their surfaces. The complexity of machinery, the betrayal of the economy, the delusion of all that had been the 20's inspired a return to the basics. The new ideal was simplicity. The task of the designer, whether he be designer of buildings or of kitchen toasters, was to enclose in such a way as to simplify. The new packaging form was the teardrop, sleek and uncomplicated; the look was horizontal; the line was the parabolic curve, the Streamline.

Building materials were chosen for their adaptability to streamlining. Stucco, because it could be smoothly molded, was particularly popular. It provided a sculptured, plain surface, and was generally light in tone in keeping with the model of clean efficiency. Bricks and cement blocks could also be arranged in such a way as to achieve a flow. New materials such as vitrolite, carrara, and shiny porcelain were applied to produce instant sleekness. Glass blocks were used extensively, inside and out.

The advent of steel frame construction meant that the corner, formerly load-bearing, could be opened and cut in. Corner windows were wrapped around the buildings. The "ribbon window" was thus created, further emphasizing the horizontality of the building.

Thirties buildings were stretched into a streamline, with curves replacing the angles. "We are rounding the corner," punned the noted furniture designer Kem Weber in 1936, poking fun at both the basic shape of the decade and its salutary effect on the struggling economy.[1]

In 1927, two separate but related episodes altered American industry. Competition from other automobile manufacturers forced Henry Ford to look at his dully reliable Model-T and to find it out-dated. To stimulate sales he needed to be able to offer the public something new. Thus the box-like Model-T was relegated to vintage ranks, and the sleeker Model-A came into being.

At the same time Norman Bel Geddes opened his studio of industrial design. Walter Dorwin Teague followed suit with his own studio shortly after Geddes, and the concept of industrial design was born. Famous for his theatrical set designs, Geddes was the designer of the first streamlined ocean liner and is regarded as the founder of the industrial design movement. In 1939 he designed the Futurama Exhibit at the New York World's Fair.

Industrial design may have been the one business that was helped rather than hindered by the Depression. Economic necessity forced changes in design philosophy. Mass-producers had to consider new styles in order to compete. The industrial designer, with his schemes for "packaging" the product, became an integral part of product development. His was a specialized talent, that of artist and engineer and modern day medicine man. American engineering and abstract art coalesced into industrial design. The designer first had to understand the machine and its dynamics and then he had to persuade the public taste with his artistic sense.

Aero-dynamics stirred the imaginations of the designers. The airplane was necessarily devoid of ornament and formed in harmony with the airflow. Aero-dynamics were applied first to the transportation forms, and the public embraced the new symbol for moving ahead. Ships, trains and automobiles borrowed the curved look from the airplane. The "Streamline," a word contributed to the everyday vocabulary by Norman Bel Geddes, became a design byword. It became the sign and symbol of the new freedom in space, the exponent of modernity in all things.

Geddes suggested that 20th Century Americans were not masters of the machine but its victims. The best designs in his eyes were those suited exclusively to their purpose. Appearance should express function, not disguise it. It was the role of the industrial designer to make peace with the machine and to glorify it.

Factories began to be viewed as "machines" for the machines. Commercial architecture borrowed the Streamline of the transportation machines. In 1931 Geddes projected the "House of Tomorrow," a streamlined residence. The home, according to Geddes, was a "machine for living."

The machine, and particularly the transportation machine, became a symbol of escape from the Depression. The architecture reflected it in the completely new style buildings that began to dot the face of the nation. These buildings were oriented to the automobile. Diners, forerunners of the fast food chains, and service stations were developed for the customer on the road. Life began to keep pace with the faster modes of transportation.

Sometime in the 20's the idea of "packaging" service stations was conceived. Steel frame construction and new lightweight materials for facades made factory production feasible. The gas station escalated in importance as the automobile became a major part of American life.

By the early 30's many of the major oil companies had become interested in the advantages of standardizing their stations. A standard design that could be recognized from a fast-moving car would not only have trademark value, but would be efficient in terms of sales, service, and merchandizing. It cost less to reproduce standardized stations, an important factor during depressed times. With more than twenty-one different oil companies represented by service stations, Tulsa in the 30's was fertile ground for a number of marketing innovations.

A September, 1931 article in *National Petroleum News* reported that Cities Service Company had a new type of service station which used a standardized main building design, color scheme, and building material. Ideas for the station originated at a sales meeting of the marketing divisions in Toronto in November, 1929. Plans were later developed by architects and engineers.

The Cities Service stations were of white terra cotta tile with a base of black tile that footed the buildings from the foundations to the sills of the display windows. The steeply pitched roofs were of black and white enameled metal tile. Green was used on the wings. It was a trademark, advertising the company's green "Koolmotor" gasoline. The distinguishing features of the stations were the two octagonal glass tower display windows. Vertical black bands accentuated the height of the towers in the 20's style.

The Cities Service stations designed at the beginning of the 30's reflected the 20's architecture. Less than five years later other oil companies demonstrated a commitment to the Streamline. The vertical lines disappeared and the roofs were flattened. The Shell Petroleum Corporation became part of this 30's trend.

They announced in the July-August, 1935 issue of the *Shell Globe* that they had just completed nine porcelain enamel service station buildings in the modern style. Impressed with the Chicago World's Fair 1933-34 Century of Progress buildings which were simple and bold, Shell chose to emulate their architectural philosophy. The Shell stations were horizontal boxes, flat-roofed, with slightly rounded corners. To give a brisk, business appearance, they were designed devoid of cornices or projecting surfaces. By the time of the Shell design most designers of service stations recognized their significance as an expression of modern civilization.

In order to stimulate the economy and attract consumers, products had to appear new and modern. With so much competition for so few available dollars, commercial marketing became big business. Alternatives to cash money were tested, and the credit card system, which was an innovation of the gasoline marketing minds, forever revolutionized America's spending patterns.

A logical outgrowth of the packaging of the new stations was a movement to "dress up" older stations. The following recommendations for updating reflect the modern mode: flood lighting; flattening the roof; increasing the window space; landscaping; and a color change that was clean-looking, but not brilliant.

Signs were another marketing device. A 1930 article in *Petroleum Age,* titled "All the Dope on Signs for Stations," emphasized the importance of signs. Their potential as "silent salesman" was beginning to be realized.

Neon tubing became popular because it was associated with "modern" and it was more brilliant than the standard incandescent bulb. It gave a smooth glow that could be seen for long distances. Although it was 40 per cent more expensive at the outset, it was much cheaper to operate.

The Parisian influence extended even to neon. The world's first neon-lit advertising sign was exhibited in a Paris motor show in 1910 by Georges Claude, a French chemist. The first World War delayed its promotion, and patents were not given until 1915. By 1923 industries had been set up in France, Canada, Australia, and the United States.

Federal Electric in Chicago obtained the patent rights to manufacture and sell neon tubing in the U.S. and had a branch office in Tulsa under the name of Claude Neon Federal by 1928. Within ten years neon was widely used in signs.

Neon gas is illuminated by an electric charge passing through it, causing it to glow red. Argon gas, also colorless, glows blue when electrified. Other colors are obtained through blending either of these gases with colored tubing. Neon, of course, is confined to tubing, but interesting effects can be had by twisting the tubing in a serpentine fashion. In the 30's, giant snakes of neon appeared to be wiggling down the new commercial strips that had begun to develop for the auto-oriented society.

The steel frame was the forerunner of the pre-fabricated building as it had been the forerunner of the skyscraper of the 20's. Walls could be hung anywhere and fitted like a skin over the steel skeleton. The framework bore the weight of the structure. The "packaged" service stations were constructed of lightweight angle frame steel and fabricated with porcelain or sheet metal in units of suitable sizes. Because the fabrication could be done in a shop, the field labor required for erection was greatly reduced. The time required to put together a prefabricated

CITIES SERVICE CIRCA 1933

BLACK GLASS MID-CONTINENT CIRCA 1931

station was about one-third that of masonry constructed stations. Five men could erect the frame-work in a single day.

Along with speed of construction, prefabrication had another decided advantage. Stations built in this manner were 95 per cent salvageable and thus could be moved with little loss of initial investment. In the 30's such portability was a highly desirable factor. Expiration of leases was a continuing problem, but property owners had much less clout when they found that the oil companies could "fold their tents and silently steal away." Poor planning or a change in traffic patterns could often place a station in a bad location. The prefabricated station could be moved instead of written off.

Porcelain panels became popular in the construction of prefabricated service stations. As a material, porcelain had certain inherent advantages. It was fireproof. It allowed uniformity of design as well as flexibility in the architecture. Because porcelain could be made in many bright colors, there were an infinite number of possible color combinations. The bright and shiny surface cleaned easily and was ideal for illumination.

The 30's was a decade of alloys, steel, plastic and glass. These included materials such as vitrolite, bakelite, carrara, vitaglass, chrome, aluminum and monel. Probably the most widely used glass product of the time was glass block or glass brick. Although it had no strength as a building material, glass block had good insulating qualities. It was an extremely versatile material and dazzling theatrical effects could be achieved with it. A wall of glass block admitted light which was diffused and refracted. Images were broken into abstract segments. Viewed from the exterior, the blocks had a sparkling crystalline quality.

A variety of sizes and shapes were available. Blocks were manufactured by the glass companies in standard sizes of 4″ x 4″, 6″ x 6″, 8″ x 8″, and one foot square. They were 4″ thick. Curved blocks, and corner blocks were available and were ideal for creating the Streamline effect. The blocks were popular commercially and residentially and were used inside and out.

MARATHON CIRCA 1933

Vitrolite and cararra were structural glass materials first used in Tulsa in the early 30's. The difference between the two was imperceptible in terms of appearance. Vitrolite, produced by Libby Owens Ford, was a rolled material. Consequently, it tended to have a wavy appearance. Cararra, probably named for the pure white marble, was a ground and polished material made by Pittsburgh Plate Glass. The polishing made it less wavy than vitrolite, but it was produced under so much heat that it was extremely difficult to keep the color constant. Cararra was used more extensively in Tulsa because Pittsburgh Plate Glass had many sales representatives in the area. Cararra and vitrolite are no longer manufactured. Their popularity was relatively short-lived, spanning just about twenty years.

A prototype of the Streamline filling station was developed in Tulsa in the early 30's and built in Sapulpa, Oklahoma for Mid-Continent Petroleum Corporation. It originated as a black glass (vitrolite) station. During a trip to Cincinnati in the late 20's, the head of marketing for Mid-Continent, Douglas Wixson, saw a service station faced with black glass. He believed that such a station would be a wonderful marketing gimmick and that black glass would be a convenient material for service stations. In 1931 he asked his friend, Donald McCormick, architect (1898-), if he could design such a building. McCormick, beginning to feel the pinch of the Depression in the building industry, was delighted. Remembering those Depression days in Tulsa, he said, "It drove you crazy when you had work, and you were mad all the time when you didn't. During the Depression, the commercial building business went flat. Only the independent oil men had money. I did large residences, and that kept me going. And I played a lot of chess!"

The original black glass station was superlative. It featured the Mid-Continent logo etched into the walls above the doors and trimmed in cream and red, the company's colors. The logo was repeated on the gas pumps, which were also covered in black glass. The building itself was composed of two parts, one housing the office and the other the service department. The diamond emblem projected above the roofline of the office portion of

SKELLY CIRCA 1938

the building. Windows were in the front and on the exposed side of the office to allow greater visibility for the attendant. The modernistic building was anchored by vertical piers.

The use of black glass was unusual and attracted attention. At least one other black glass station was built from this design in Kansas City, Missouri. The glass designed station was later produced in cream porcelain with red and black trim. These stations were prefabricated in a Tulsa shop. One of them was built in Tulsa at the corner of 21st Street and Utica Avenue. Many others sprang up all over the midwest, in Indiana, Iowa, Kansas, and Missouri. In fact, the station became so well identified with Mid-Continent that miniatures were made to use as promotions at trade fairs.

Marathon Oil Company was also represented in Tulsa. In 1933 they built a unique geometric station at the corner of Brady and Boston Avenues just one block from the new Union Train Depot. The building was an octagon, 18 feet in diameter, constructed of white enameled brick, with a metal roof. A stepped dome with the trademark "Marathon Runner" at the top was a distinguishing feature and part of the signage. Both dome and runner were of cast aluminum. Skelly Oil and Standard Oil (Stanolind) also experimented with standardized stations in the 30's.

A coalition of architecture and industrial design took place in Walter Dorwin Teague's service station design for Texaco. The Texas Oil Company became convinced that the new field of industrial design held the solution to standardized designs for service stations. In 1936 they hired Teague, one of the best-known industrial designers. Teague viewed the role of industrial design as a method of organizing a product to increase its appeal and hence its sales. The thrust of this as he saw it, was to sell the product. The service stations were designed as sales packages.

Teague and his designers undertook an extensive survey to draw up the guidelines for the Texaco design. Primary requirements such as trademark and color standardization, efficient layout for sales and adequate office and rest room space were obvious. Teague concluded that the major considerations in the standardized design were comfort and merchandizing. Cleanliness, the selection of materials that could be kept clean, the use of space to eliminate messy service operations from waiting areas, and the inclusion of a canopy in the design for the protection of the customer were all comfort factors essential to a good design. The psychological subtleties involved in merchandizing through design were less apparent. Speed in servicing was important and should be increased by creating greater visibility from the manager's office. Accessibility to the station itself and its merchandise was necessary to the customer. Effective night lighting should be incorporated into the design to promote night business. Large display areas advantageously placed would bring the merchandise to the customer. A concentration of sales appeal at the pumps should be included in the space allotments. Thus the prominent displays of oil cans and tires were the result of merchandizing psychology.

Teague developed a standardized design with five major variations. These were dependent in part upon lot limitations. His designs could be adapted to the use of different building materials within the various geographical regions. Teague's design, featuring smooth surfaces and round sweeping corners, conveyed the aero-dynamic imagery. The three bands of color stripes, sweeping around the buildings became a hallmark of the Streamline style. Red stars, the Texaco emblem, were placed evenly above the bands, and bold red lettering was set off by the white background. The "packaging" of the service station into a streamlined form culminated with Teague's design for Texaco.

It has been said that the diner is an American art form, which could be why some critics have had considerable reservations about American art. Nonetheless, the *Wall Street Journal*, March 28, 1980, dignified the Streamlined White Tower hamburger diners, among others, in an article by William M. Bulkeley, "To Preserve or Not? That Is the Question For a Neo-Neon Age." The article noted that "A scattering of preservationists and architectural

SOUTHWEST BOULEVARD TEXACO CIRCA 1980

historians all over the country are increasingly developing an appreciation for roadside diners and motels, hot-dog stands and neon signs, auto dealerships and Depression-era drugstores — the sorts of commercial designs that are . . . usually found along the commercial 'strips' outside American cities."

Steven Izenour, a Philadelphia architect, collaborated on a book about the White Tower hamburger stands because he was interested in "the way they'd strip off the skin every few years and put on a new one to reflect subtle shifts in popular taste."[2] Tulsa's distant relative to the White Tower diners was called "Silver Castle." Its name was taken from the "White Castle" in Wichita, Kansas. The first Silver Castle opened at 15th Street and Peoria Avenue in the spring of 1936. Eight more were built in Tulsa, and scattered ones cropped up in various parts of the Southwest.

The first buildings came from a sectional building company in Wichita. Later, J. W. McCollum and I. H. Parkey, the partners who operated Silver Castle, started the Castle Fixture Company and built their own buildings. They sold a variety of restaurant supplies as well, from booths and stools to cups and saucers.

The diners were designed by a draftsman for the fixture company. Diners were rarely designed by architects. They were often prefabricated, like the service stations. This standardization within a given chain not only cut down building costs, but served as a "sign" that the public could recognize.

The Silver Castle diners were of two designs. One was very simple, but eye catching, which made it desirable as a roadside beacon. The building was a plain box shape covered with porcelain panels that were separated by silver chromium strips. Porcelain panels composed the interior surfaces as well.

The second and more popular style developed as a Streamline building with a crowning stepped roof above the curved facade of the building. These structures were sectional steel, painted silver with a sand finished paint to give the illusion and texture of stucco. The windows were shaded by black and white striped awnings. The overall color scheme was silver, black, and white. The silver and chromium interior consisted of a counter and Pullman booths.

TILE EXTERIOR CIRCA 1940

PORCELAIN EXTERIOR CIRCA 1940

INTERIOR

BLACK GLASS EXTERIOR

A movement to "modernize Main Street" was a natural outgrowth of the Depression and the need to lure buyers with new, modern, up-to-date, forward-looking goods. There was little money to spend, yet merchants and financial institutions needed to do something to attract customers. The least expensive way to update was to create a modern facade. This was often done, in the most prosaic of terms, by the mere addition of porcelain, vitrolite, cararra. These materials could give a sleek new look relatively inexpensively. Aluminum banding could be wrapped around, covering seams, and leading the eye to the building's updated lines.

Security Federal Savings and Loan (now the Court of Three Sisters) is an example of this kind of 30's modernization. Tulsa's growing pains are felt in its condensed history, spanning a little over a decade from the early 20's to the mid-30's. Security Federal began as a small, but prosperous concern, providing residential loans in Tulsa. The Depression was devastating to the home loan business, but Security Federal was able to weather it through with some help. The help came in part from William G. Skelly, owner of the Skelly Building, where Security Federal rented space. Skelly repeatedly lowered their rent during the 30's so that the Savings and Loan could meet the payments for their office space. In 1932 they were paying $1900 for a six month lease. By 1935 the cost had been reduced to only $600 for the six months.

In 1937 the Tulsa business climate had vastly improved, and downtown rentals became more expensive. Security Federal's rent was increased to $1200 for six months. The bank's board members agreed to investigate other less costly alternatives. Within the month the purchase of a building at 120 W. 4th Street had been approved.

The building was purchased for $8,000 with an additional $4,500 allocated for its remodeling. Harry Mahler (1876-1975), was hired to do the necessary architectural design work. Mahler had worked in Chicago for the firm of Holabird and Roche from 1898-1918. While in Chicago he lived across the street from Frank Lloyd Wright, and they became friends. He left Chicago to work in Tulsa as an engineer for Oklahoma Iron Works and soon set up his own architectural practice.

Mahler's job was to update a basic brick building. He faced the one story structure with black vitrolite panels, alternately dull and polished, creating a checkerboard effect. Single vertical piers rise slightly at either end of the building. Another pair of vertical piers flank the entrance in a stepped back design that terminates in a peak. Horizontal bands of aluminum accentuate the roof line and the vertical piers. A clock is contained in the peak, suggesting a pediment, while the Greek design etched into the vitrolite at the top of the four main piers adds another traditional element to the otherwise thoroughly "modern" building.

The 30's modernization of Main Street can still be seen in the Lerner Shop building located between 4th and 5th Streets on Main. Built in the early 1900's by pioneer bankers Lee Clinton and Samuel P. McBirney, it was a simple two-story red brick building. For many years a music company rented the first floor and the second floor functioned as a rooming house. In the mid-30's the Lerner Shops leased the building and remodeled its facade in the Streamline style of the decade.

As the movement to modernize Main Street progressed, the cost of downtown space escalated. Many businesses could not afford the increase and looked for other alternatives. One alternative was found in the less expensive real estate in the suburbs and along the fast-developing strips.

Tulsa's first outlying shopping center, Whittier Square, developed in the early 30's at Admiral Boulevard and Lewis Avenue where the trolley stopped. Although Whittier Square was conveniently located near public transportation, it was oriented to the automobile. It was set off from the road by a space devoted to automobile parking. Customer entrances opened onto the parking lot. Signage was auto-directed and signs were bigger. The bright glow of neon attracted the attention of motorists.

As the decade drew to a close, Whittier Square merchants wanted to offer convenient banking facilities to their customers. In 1938 the Bank of Red Fork was persuaded to move into the area. It was renamed the People's State Bank. In 1941 they leased and remodeled a building at 2408 East Admiral, which had originally been an A & P grocery, later a skating rink, and finally the office of the American Insurance Company.

In most instances commercial Streamline modernization took place without an architect. The building facades were left to the devices of the glass companies and their sales representatives. So it was in this case. Dyke Brothers Glass Company was contacted to modernize the People's State Bank. It was designed totally by the sales representative. Prior to the remodeling, the building was an undistinguished, flat-roofed, brick structure. It is now sheathed in black vitrolite.

Black glass was not only an easy solution to the outward modernization of an older building, it was also, as in Mid-Continent's prototype service station, a popular material for a totally new building. Whitlock's Grocery Store was a new brick building with a black glass facade chosen because Whitlock thought it would make "a nice modern front." It had always been his dream to build his own grocery store, and he wanted his 1937 building to reflect the modern times. The front of the store was devoted to customer space, and designed using long ceiling beams for support instead of pillars, which would have interfered with the floor space. Large display windows on either side of the center door were shaded by metal awnings.

Before building their new store on 11th Street, the Whitlocks owned and operated a smaller store on South College Avenue. The new store was the first in Tulsa to use cellophane wrapping and was particularly known for its bakery which produced 4,000 to 5,000 pounds of fruit cake a year.

In 1936 the Tulsa Monument Company followed the trend to the suburbs. Harry H. Mahler, the architect who remodeled Security Federal's building, suggested that the monument company's new building simulate the appearance of a monument. The result is a handsome resolution of the sometimes ridiculous "Coney Island" architecture that dotted the strips with buildings disguised as hot dogs and donuts.

A long building, the Tulsa Monument Company contains both horizontal and vertical elements. It is composed

TILE AND GLASS BLOCK EXTERIOR

BLACK GLASS EXTERIOR CIRCA 1948

BLACK GLASS EXTERIOR

of exactly symmetrical wings which extend on either side of the main entrance. It is a single-story, flat roofed building of white plaster concrete trimmed in gunmetal gray. Vertical lines are in the clock tower and the pillars that extend slightly above the roof line at the corners of the building. The pillars are square and outlined at the top by three horizontal gray bands. The same three bands of gray above the entrance create a canopy illusion.

The central focus is the tall clock tower over the main entrance with spot-lighted clocks on three sides. The tower is stepped back and flanked by vertical pillars identical to those that mark the corners. The tower treatment lends a monumental quality to the building. Its verticality is accented by columns of glass brick inset in a narrow perpendicular line.

The solidity of the architecture contrasts with the improvised beginnings of the company. Although it is one of the ten oldest industries in Tulsa, its beginning was a fluke. It is a descendent of a tombstone company that had been operated by L. G. West in Tulsa in 1896. West was the landlord for an Italian marble company salesman. One day the man paid his room and board, and announced that he would be gone for some time on a collecting trip. He left behind a substantial supply of gravestone samples. The salesman never returned. After quite a wait, West grew tired of storing the materials and started disposing of the gravestones. It was then that he realized the future in the monument business.

With the commercial move toward the suburban areas, it was profitable to offer other services to residents who enjoyed the convenience of shopping and doing business in their own neighborhoods. In 1942, the City Veterinary Clinic bought property on the commercial strip of the Brookside residential neighborhood.

The City Veterinary Clinic (1942) was built in the Streamline commercial style of many of the veterinary hospitals of the era. It is a one-story buff brick building with rounded Streamline corners. It makes extensive use of glass block, which composes the curved entrance as well as the curved corners of the building itself. The building has a flat roof with a banded parapet and a curved canopy above the entrance.

Joseph R. Kobering, the architect, and Dr. William F. Irwin, the client, looked at a number of other veterinary hospitals before they planned the building. A functional design, it is still in operation as a veterinary hospital.

Movies, America's tastemaker for the modern life, reflected changes in communication in the 30's the way television did in the 50's. An escape from the reality of the Depression, they brought a totally new element of information, taste, and culture to the masses. For Oklahomans, the movie theaters with their "refrigeration," also offered an escape from the heat and the dust of the terrible Dust Bowl summers in the mid-30's. Hollywood portrayed the modern lifestyle in a fantasy of song and dance. Ginger Rogers and Fred Astaire danced on a bakelite stage, chosen because it was slick, shiny, and reflective; agonizing to choreograph because the surface scratched so badly that it had to be polished every few steps.

Hollywood put the good guys in white hats and the bad guys in black ones. It put the good girls in rooms full of chintz covered furniture and hooked rugs while the bad girls lounged on sleek chrome chaises in mirrored boudoirs, plushly carpeted in white. The suggestions of the screen regarding styles, manners and taste in furniture and art, did not go unnoticed.

The Palace Theater, on Main Street, was an example of the move to "modernize Main Street" in the mid-30's. Formerly the Wonderland, it was one of Tulsa's oldest amusement places. In 1935 it was announced that the Palace would undergo a complete modernization of its exterior. Interior modernization was planned for sometime in the future. "Modernized Main Street" was enthusiastically accepted by the *Tulsa World* in an article on March 10, 1935: "When the exterior modernization is completed, property owners in the block on South Main . . . in the older section of the business district can visualize what it would mean to their properties to make such an improvement . . . It is the most important modernization program announced . . . thus far this year . . . ."

SOUTH EXTERIOR

Joseph R. Koberling, designer of some of Tulsa's first Art Deco buildings, was the architect for the remodeling of the Palace. The facade was extended with metal lath and stucco of a light buff color. A metal marquee was added to provide space for signage and a shelter from the weather. The modernization was not extreme. It was tentative. The materials of the 30's were incorporated into Zigzag elements of the late 20's and into conservative elements of the PWA.

Three years after the modernization of the Palace, theater streamlining arrived in the form of the Delman Theater at 15th Street and Lewis Avenue. The Delman was committed lock, stock, and barrel to the Streamline. It is a symmetrical white stucco rectangle broken with broad stepping. The box office was originally in the middle of the building until a car rearranged it a bit in the 50's.

The Delman theater was part of a chain of theaters built by I. B. Adelman of Beverly Hills, California. He built four theaters from the same plans in Tulsa, Wichita, Dallas, and Houston. The architect, W. Scott Dunne, was from Dallas.

Adelman was considered a pioneer in "deluxe" neighborhood theater operations. Major movie houses and large theaters had been confined to the downtown area until the 30's. The Delman was the largest capacity movie house in Tulsa when it was built. Its "slide-back" chairs were new to theaters in the Southwest. The interior fixtures were Deco. A curved double metal railing and stepped bannister led to the huge balcony. The original white stucco walls with battlement designs have been replaced by draped walls.

The Will Rogers Theater, built in 1941, is similar in style to the many white stucco theater buildings constructed in California in the late 30's. The front of the building faces the corner of the street, and is concave, a complement to the cylindrical island ticket booth. A Streamline marquee extends from the building beyond the

EAST EXTERIOR

ticket booth. A tower soars above the marquee, directly over the ticket booth, resembling a lighthouse tower. It provides a sign for the theater. "Will Rogers" is spelled out vertically in bold neon letters.

The pavement in front of the building has a colored geometric pattern further accentuating the curve of the building. Broad bands of alternating red and buff concrete extend the curved outline to the sidewalk, abruptly turning the corner with the building. In a semi-circle in front of the ticket booth the concrete bands become wedge shapes that radiate to the curb. The sidewalk gives the illusion of being a continuation of the theater lobby. Built by Griffith Southwest Theaters, the architects were Jack Corgan and W. J. Moore, both of Dallas. E. K. Schmeusser did the interior artistry, the painting of Will Rogers in the lobby, and the carvings of the Rogers' family that decorate the side walls.

The theater opened as a "subsequent run" movie house, playing films after their downtown first run. The opening show in 1941 was "Mr. and Mrs. Smith," starring Carole Lombard and Robert Montgomery. Admission prices were twenty cents and four mils for adults, and ten cents and two mils for children. Will Rogers Theater operated until August 25, 1977, the forty-second anniversary of Will's death. Population shifts and fewer available films forced the closing of the theater.

Movies provided the vision in the 20's and 30's, but the day to day influence was in the sound of the radio. Radio was *the* new form of communication in the 20's. By 1920, manufacturers of radio supplies began to furnish programs to promote their products, and commercial radio broadcasting was born. In the 30's radio came into its own as a communication and advertising tool. Roosevelt began his "fireside chats" with the nation. Mass media, with all its political and marketing implications, came into being.

KVOO started in 1924 in Bristow, Oklahoma, as a small radio station with the call letters KRFU. Sometime

ARCHITECTURAL RENDERING FROM
NEWSPAPER PLATE

EXTERIOR CIRCA 1948

EXTERIOR CIRCA 1952

in the 20's F. J. Laux, a Bristow attorney, named the station the "Voice of Oklahoma," and the call letters were changed to correspond. In 1927 the station was purchased by a group of Tulsans, led by William G. Skelly, and it was moved to Tulsa. It became an NBC affiliate the same year. About a year later, KVOO was in financial trouble, and Skelly bought it from his partners and took control of the management.

    Early day listeners recall artists like Bob and Johnny Lee Wills, Gene Autry, Will Rogers, and Jimmy Wilson's "Catfish String Band" on the "Voice of Oklahoma."

    KVOO's original power plant was on "Reservoir Hill." Power boosts were granted by the Federal Radio Commission (later the Federal Communications Commission), and by the end of 1932, Skelly had purchased a Western Electric 50,000 Watt transmitter with permission to operate at half capacity. The 11th Street Transmitter Station was built to contain this new equipment.

    Built by John T. Blair (1885-1976), the architect who had designed Skelly's home, the transmitter station is a pale version of what was originally planned. The rendering of the original design bears many similarities to the Tulsa

EXTERIOR CIRCA 1940

Fire Alarm Building in site and style. The transmitter station as it was built is a concrete structure, one and a half stories above ground, with the main entrance up a short flight of stairs. The tall, narrow windows on all sides of the building are now covered. Almost fifty years later the structure is still in use as a transmitter station.

As cost factors forced commercial businesses to flee toward the outlying areas, so residential building moved farther from the downtown. Very little major commercial building took place in the mid-30's until the government began to share in the cost. Custom building was residential, and it was limited to the elite few who had money to spend.

"One trouble with the improperly organized house
is that there is not enough opportunity
for people to see less of each other."

—*Norman Bel Geddes*

"We enter a new era. Are we ready for the changes that are coming? The houses we live in tomorrow will not much resemble the houses we live in today. Automobiles, railway trains, theatres, cities, industry itself, are undergoing rapid changes. Likewise, art in all its forms . . . We live and work under pressure with a tremendous expenditure of energy. We feel that life in our time is more urgent, complex and discordant than life ever was before. That may be so. In the perspective of fifty years hence, the historian will detect in (this) decade . . . a period of tremendous significance. He will see it as a period of criticism, unrest, and dissatisfaction to the point of disillusion—when new aims were being sought and new beginnings were astir."[3]

Norman Bel Geddes wrote that passage in 1932 as the beginning of his book, *Horizons.* We are the historians "in the perspective of fifty years hence," and his comments are relevant today.

Geddes postulated that the "house should be a factory for living." The difficulty with the house as it was being traditionally built according to Geddes was that the architects were still trying to fit new patterns into old styles. Inconvenience and cramping resulted. Applied ornament in the style of Colonial, Norman or Tudor was expensive as was the wasted space of attic and basement. Like a factory, the modern house should develop as the result of an interior plan. The traditional residential floor plan was almost reversed. Instead of an impressive lawn in front of the house with the interior living space at the front, Geddes proposed that services should be in the front with living areas in the rear.

The siting of the house was a major consideration. Modern houses were designed to be approached by auto, and the housing of the auto became an integral part of the plan. Thus the garage was located at the front of the house, and the house located close to the street. By siting the house at the front of its property line, an unbroken, parklike setting was created at the back of the house for play and garden space. Living areas located at the back overlooked the yard. Room exposures were considered too; sleeping rooms, for example, required air and sun.

According to Geddes, the incentive "to get out of the house" was the result of the inhabitants being thrown together constantly. Therefore the house should have space for six times the number of people normally living in it. It was essential to have quiet, private nooks and separate places for older and younger people. Every member of the family needed to have a place where he could be by himself, and a library was essential. Playrooms for children, as well as the playroom for adults, the living room, should have unbroken spaciousness for flexible use.

The steel frame construction did not define and limit partitioning as did the traditional masonry wall forms. The second story walls did not have to correspond to the walls on the first floor. Then too, more space could be allowed for windows. Windows or glass doors could extend from floor to ceiling or from partition to partition. Finally, the new flat roof provided terrace space. Pitched roofs were obsolete.

Streamlining had begun as a commercial movement. The rationale behind its extension into residential architecture poses many questions, and provokes endless speculation. Tradition dictated applied ornamentation and decoration to achieve the inviting warmth of a home. Yet functional necessity was the *raison d'etre* of a Streamline house. Consequently, many viewed the structures as stark and cold. One might suggest that modern families built Streamline residences because: they felt the need to simplify their lives and grasped at the Streamline home as a solution; or they wished to rebel from the constraints of the time and chose to stamp their personalities on something unique; or those who could afford to build during the Depression had more money than taste; or they liked to shock people; or they were more advanced in their conception of functional values; or the women chose the home's design. Certainly the builders of Streamline residences had more in common than home builders of any other time. The Depression was the unifying factor. Tulsans who could afford to build had managed to remain in a privileged position.

Whatever the reasons, it is important to realize just how different these homes were at that time and how many were built in Tulsa. Very little custom building was being done in the midst of the Depression, and yet a city the size of Tulsa produced nearly a dozen Streamline residences. Tulsa was a young city, appealing to the adventurous spirit. It is perhaps logical that the houses built during this depressed time were very modern. It may have been an attempt to break with the past.

The streamlining of the houses did not follow the ovoid aerodynamic. It was streamlining in terms of simplicity and horizontality. The houses utilized transportation imagery borrowed from the steamship. Houses appeared as floating ships on the rolling hills of Tulsa's residential neighborhoods. Terrace spaces were transformed into ship's decks with ship's railings. Occasionally there were ladders from "lower" to "upper" decks. Porthole windows were used. All of the Streamline houses built in Tulsa in the 30's, however, have traditional features seldom found in today's modern homes.

The J. B. McGay residence is the house that the parking meter built. Inventor of a tubeless tire, a gas calculator, and various gauges, McGay invented the parking meter in 1934. He built his house two years later. The McGay residence is a maverick, designed by Joseph R. Koberling. The house was considered very unusual at the time for its corner windows, front garage, and five different levels. The house is made of traditional materials, white painted brick and green wrought iron Spanish-style window balconies. The scale of the house is large and incorporates elements of the early Zigzag style. There are vertical elements in the massing, and the wrought iron work under the windows tends to elongate them. The ironwork on the balconies and the geometrically designed panel inserts above the front windows break the otherwise severe front facade.

The verticality of the house is juxtaposed with the long horizontal line, achieved by attaching the garage to one side of the facade and extending a garden wall on the opposite side. The center section of the house has a modified pitched roof, while the extending wings are flat-roofed. A cantilevered canopy covers the front entrance. The back windows look onto a curved patio.

The design for the McGay house originated as part of a folder of sketches that Koberling had made of different styles of houses to interest prospective clients. This was during the depth of the Depression before the government building projects had gotten underway. The architects were all struggling to find work.

The house has a staggered floor plan with split levels. The living room is several steps down from the entry and a recreation room is on the next level below. The two levels above the entrance are bedrooms. An etched glass mirror sets off the living room fireplace, and a geometric floral design decorates the mantle. The same mantle

1551 SOUTH YORKTOWN PLACE

treatment is found in the master bedroom. The bathrooms have carrara structural glass wainscoting. The master bath is soft green tile accented with black glass. A corbelled arch, outlined in black glass, leads to the shower. McGay designed and fabricated his own stair rail of sleek, monel metal. The interior materials of the house are much less traditional than the exterior, suggesting an acceptance of the modern in terms of every day life style.

One of the architects for Webster High School, William H. Wolaver, designed the Theodore N. Law house, built in 1935. The house was Wolaver's first excursion into modern design. Law says that the house was his wife's project. She was committed to making it completely modern throughout, even traveling to New York with the architect to find the appropriate fixtures. Wolaver remembers that they picked out everything—from ceiling fixtures to flatware and bath towels.

The house is sited forward on its lot. A circular drive leads to the canopied front entrance, which has a theatrical appearance. Genevieve Hodge Law was the daughter of William Hodge, Sr., a Broadway actor, and her mother and sister were also in Broadway productions. The entry is sheltered by a dramatic concrete canopy. The front door is stepped back into a recess. Windows are large, and surfaces are plain, lending a starkness to the overall theme. A circular opening cut out of the side of the canopy offers a balance to the large second story multi-paned porthole window. The garage and porte cochere to the side repeat the porthole motif.

A two-story house, it is made of brick that is lightly plastered and painted white. Designed on a center hall plan with two main wings, the east wing is a cylindrical projection with curved casement windows. The west wing wraps around the side of the house in a curve of glass block and casement ribbon windows. Expansive central living areas flow into smaller and more intimate rooms. The many, large windows allow the outside in. The size of the house is more apparent from the rear, where it is composed of many levels of projecting rectangular wings, broken by a curved wall. A back staircase leads to the flat roof.

Theodore N. Law came to Tulsa in 1934 and organized Falcon Seaboard Drilling Company. In addition to his oil interests, he was very involved in aviation, serving as a director of Mid-Continent Airlines, Inc. and Braniff International Airways. He was also a vice president and director of U.S. Airlines, Inc. and served as the president of

MONEL METAL RAILING

CORBELLED ARCH IN BATH

1841 EAST 27TH STREET

ENTRANCE

GLASS BAY

Alaska Airlines for a short time in 1945. An advisor for Aerovies Latina Americanas and President of Aero Exploration Company, he was considered an expert on Latin America and spoke at Tulsa's Philbrook Art Museum on the subject. His civic involvements were as wide-ranging as were his business interests, which extended north to Alaska and south to Latin America.

Another Streamline residence was designed by Leo Clark for Arnold Ungerman, a doctor specializing in neurology. From 1937-1938 Ungerman worked for the United States Department of Indian Affairs as a consulting neurologist and neuropsychiatrist on a Hopi-Navaho reservation. At that time he and his wife, an attorney, fell in love with the Southwestern style of architecture. The house they built for themselves in 1941 was intended to be a blend of Mexican-Southwestern and contemporary modern. It is a two-story concrete block structure on a concrete slab foundation. A curved canopy shelters the recessed door. The house features a flat roof, corner windows, and a curved bay composed of glass block. Horizontal bands above the entry and at the roof line add to the Streamline effect. The interior plan is traditional with modern finishings and hardware. The door handles are all of soft brushed aluminum, and the stair rail is solid copper. The light fixtures were produced by Empire Chandelier of Sand Springs.

Both of the Ungermans were civically involved. He founded the first Department of Psychiatry in Oklahoma at Hillcrest Medical Center. He also helped found the Tulsa Psychiatric Foundation and established the Child Guidance Clinic at the Childrens' Medical Center.

The Burtner Fleeger residence was designed by Frederick Vance Kershner and built in 1937. It was the first monolithic concrete house in Tulsa. Portland Cement Company participated in the engineering. Walls are of reinforced poured concrete, 12-14 inches thick. The exterior is striated with narrow horizontal bands.

1718 EAST 37TH STREET

2424 EAST 29TH STREET

Fleeger was a Civil Engineer who came to Tulsa from Pittsburgh in 1926 after purchasing an interest in Oklahoma Steel Castings Company. He became president of the company in 1935. He was one of Tulsa's prominent civic as well as business leaders.

Kershner found the Fleegers "ideal" clients. They wanted something attractive and different, but gave the architect freedom in design. The house is basically modern but with a potpourri of strongly traditional elements as well. The wings are composed of intersecting rectangular blocks. The structure was designed to conform to the very uneven lot level, which sloped down in the back and on one side. Consequently, the basement, first, and second floors are all on ground level at either the front or the back. The house is massed to the highest point above the entry, with the roof levels stepped down, like a series of stairs to the garage. The garage is in the front. The flat roof is emphasized with banded lines.

Above the splayed entry is a series of three tiered windows with canopies. A classical shield motif, contained in the ironwork on the stair rail, is repeated as a decoration on the front door and on a metal panelled piece on the exterior of the house. Curved porches on the main level open as decks off the bedrooms above. Built at a time before residential air-conditioning, every bedroom was planned to open onto a deck.

The interior of the house is the same curious mixture of modern and traditional. The rooms are spacious, but arranged in the traditional pattern. The living room fireplace is of black cararra, with a curved mantle. A unique shelf design for the library includes panels which recede and allow for the addition or subtraction of bookcases. The basement features a curved bar of green glass block with a green cararra top. It is balanced by a matching glass block planter under the window.

The house that the architect, John Duncan Forsyth built in 1937 to please his wife, Ann, is a very sophisticated design. It won an Honorable Mention in a National contest by Portland Cement Company in 1937. A two-story house, it is flat roofed, and constructed of reinforced concrete on a steel frame. The original house was a pale earth pink color that had been incorporated into the concrete. Rusting of the steel caused its discoloration and it was painted. It is now white with a teal blue trim.

ENTRANCE

GLASS BLOCK BAR

Forsyth, born in Scotland, and educated in Edinburgh and Paris, was a Tulsa resident from 1925 to his death. He was one of the state's most widely known architects, his designs spanning a variety of periods and styles. Probably his most well-known design is the Will Rogers Memorial in Claremore, Oklahoma, which was chosen from nationwide competition. He was also one of the architects along with Wolaver and Kerr who was involved in the design of the Daniel Webster High School in Tulsa. Ann Forsyth was a former artist's agent from New York City. She is remembered in Tulsa as one of the founders of the Tulsa Town Hall and its original director.

The front of their house contains a massing of plain unbroken surfaces. Four inset horizontal bands divide the house evenly. The garage projects in front of the house, like a separate wing. The main entrance is sheltered on one side by the garage, its canopy curving into the garage wall.

The back of the house features great expanses of glass block. A cantilevered canopy extends to cover the second story deck. A low concrete wall affords seclusion from the street, and seems to extend as an integral part of the house.

The interior is based on a traditional floor plan. The curves of the exterior are repeated in the interior. The original furniture was modern. A Kakemono silk painting, hundreds of years old that had been given to Forsyth, remains in the living room.

Jesse Davis was a lawyer and the manager of the Long Bell Lumber Company. His wife, Frances, majored in art and was one of Adah Robinson's students. She designed their Streamline house, and a draftsman at the lumber company took her design and drew up the plans and specifications. The two-story house is constructed of brick and wood on concrete. Its prominent glass bay is suggestive of the ship imagery popular in the Streamline residences. Corner windows and horizontal ribbon windows emphasize the streamlining, and a porthole window carries out the ship motif. The back of the house has a rounded porch with a concrete deck above it that was originally edged with glass block. The deck has since been enclosed.

The most unusual element of the house is the three-story structural column of hollow fluted wood, extending from the basement through the second floor. The column is 2 feet in diameter and 26 feet high, and was the largest

2827 SOUTH BIRMINGHAM PLACE

WEST EXTERIOR

of its kind in Oklahoma at the time the house was built. It is the central feature of the house, with the entry hall staircase winding around it.

The *Tulsa World* (August 1937) included articles about the house when it was being built. Intended to be completely modern, it was the first "all electric" house in Tulsa. An open house was held the week of August 15-22, 1937, when it was completed.

Reminiscing about some of the reactions to the house, Frances Davis remembers that they were generally favorable, but people did think the house was unusual. The one remark that she recalls most clearly, because she thought it was amusing, was from a woman who said the house looked like "a pregnant elephant." The well-known contemporary houses in Tulsa at the time were Adah Robinson's and the house that Frank Lloyd Wright built for the Richard Lloyd Jones family. Frances Davis says hers is "much more simplified, of course."

In the neighborhood near the University of Tulsa is another house built in the streamlined ship style for William D. Whenthoff in 1935. It is two stories built of brick laid over tile and painted to look like stucco. There are two porthole windows, one on the first floor by the entry, the other above the entry on the second floor.

A second story balcony serves as a canopy for the entry and wraps around the house. Its triple railing creates the illusion of a ship's bridge, an illusion accented by the exterior ladder from the second floor to the flat roof. The interior of the house breaks with the modern and becomes a traditional center hall plan.

In 1937 John L. Shakely purchased almost eighty acres in the "country" to accommodate his horses and to build his home. His friend, Howard J. Sherman, bought a portion of Shakely's acreage and built his house at about the same time. This "country" property is now well within the boundaries of Tulsa's affluent residential development to the south.

THREE-STORY COLUMN

3231 SOUTH UTICA AVENUE

1142 SOUTH COLLEGE AVENUE

7219 SOUTH EVANSTON AVENUE

STAIR IN CENTRAL HALL

INFORMAL LIVING ROOM

Attracted by the oil industry, Shakely came to Tulsa from Pennsylvania in 1914. He started working in the oil field equipment supply industry for Frick-Reid Supply Corporation which was later purchased by Jones and Laughlin Supply Company. He became president of Jones and Laughlin and then president of the Oklahoma-Mississippi River Products Line, Inc. Active in civic affairs, he served as president of the Metropolitan Tulsa Chamber of Commerce and Secretary-Treasurer of the International Petroleum Exposition.

The Shakely house is a ship's house of steel reinforced concrete. A huge curved bay resembles the bow of a streamlined ship, with decks on the second story suggesting a ship's bridge with curved rail and ladder steps to the roof. A small octagonal porthole window to one side of the entry carries out the ship imagery. Horizontal bands wrap around the house just below the roof line, and ribbon windows emphasize the streamlining.

The interior is composed of large expansive rooms. A central hall banister of glass and copper spirals to the second floor. The library is curved to resemble a ship's bridge. Doors in the kitchen area have porthole windows, like a ship's galley. The upstairs bedrooms are in different wings, separating the adult area from the children's area.

The Sherman house across the street from the Shakely house is massed more vertically, but it too has open decks that are railed and is a two-story house of steel reinforced concrete. A flat roof is set off with triple pipe railing and the curved balcony on the second story is railed. A porte cochere allows automobile approach to a side door and separates the main house from the quarters. The interior of the house is composed of large rooms, each opening into the other.

Probably because they were originally "country" houses, both the Shakely and Sherman homes are sited well back on their property. Howard J. Sherman called his property "the farm" and raised turkeys there. Sherman was born in Kankakee, Illinois and came to Oklahoma to work for Phillips Petroleum in Bartlesville. He was the

FORMAL LIVING ROOM FIREPLACE

SOUTH EXTERIOR

seventeenth employee of the company and eventually became vice-president in charge of land. He left Phillips to form the firm of McIntyre-Sherman-Cummings with Paul McIntyre, the head geologist for Phillips Petroleum and Dean (C.C.) Cummings, an independent royalty broker. Sherman had an interest in the Texas Oil Field discovery of 1936.

The Streamline Art Deco style remained popular through the 40's and on into the 50's. Bevis Hillier when talking about the Art Deco of the 20's said: ". . Art Deco was a developing style. The art of the 20's was not suddenly snuffed out in 1930 with a magician's 'Now you see it, and now you don't'. Neither did all the artists die of bubonic plague in 1930. There was a strong continuity."[4]

This was true of the Streamline Art Deco architecture of the 30's. The hiatus in construction during World War II might have resulted in a complete change of style after the War. But the Streamline Art Deco was a popular and well established commercial style, and it survived. In Tulsa some late examples can be seen in the Phoenix Cleaners (1947), Morrow Geophysical Building (1948, now the American Red Cross), Midwest Marble and Tile (1945, now Type Service Corporation), the Mayo Motor Inn (1950), and the Brook Theater (1949).

7228 SOUTH EVANSTON AVENUE

▼
▼

EDITOR'S NOTE

Architecture has been called "art we walk through"—but it is more. Our built environment is a record of how we developed as a civilization. It is our past and will speak to future generations.

Historic preservation has become a popular concern in the last decade. Preservation no longer merely means restoration. While once its primary focus lay in the transformation of historic sites into public museums, now the movement's scope has broadened to include adaptive reuse of many old structures. The prerequisite that these buildings be "historically significant" no longer exists. The change that this emphasis reflects within historic preservation is a logical outgrowth for a society which is energy conscious to the point of recycling papers and aluminum cans. Historic preservationists now recognize that structures can outlive their original functions and accept the premise that architecture should meet modern needs.

We are caretakers of the past, but we are also creators of the present. New construction is one indication of a city's vitality and the balance between conservation of old buildings and construction of new is another valid measure of that vitality. The balance created should enhance the urban fabric adding richness, grace and diversity to its texture.

The popular interest in historic preservation during the last decade coincided with the revival of the 20's and 30's Art Deco. The architecture of the era developed as a romantic view of the city which reflected the hope and promise of technological wonders to come. To the architects of the day the city was an awe-inspiring celebration.

The architecture of "less is more" which followed the Art Deco movement decreed ornament a crime. The International Style built in steel and glass. Now, a half century later, functionalism no longer holds us spellbound and we seek some respite from the monotonous steel and glass boxes which populate our horizons.

The appeal of Art Deco stems in part from our increasing respect for handmade objects and our awareness of superb craftsmanship in a wide variety of materials. As Ada Louise Huxtable, architecture critic for the *New York Times* wrote in her article entitled "The Skyscraper Style": "But what is most clearly and heartbreakingly revealed in any presentation [of Art Deco architecture] is that the buildings shown represent the last great period of decorative art. We are struck by the poignant reality that it will never be possible to do this kind of work again."

Tulsa's development into a metropolitan center coincided with the emergence of Art Deco. Although over one-fourth of the buildings displaying the Zigzag style have been demolished, a significant number still remain and stand side by side examples of the International Style and the magnificent Gothic architecture of the early 1900's. It is the Art Deco structures, above all others, which define our present and offer a rich and colorful touchstone to our past.

"Architecture is to be regarded by us
with the most serious thought.
We may live without her,
and worship without her,
but we cannot remember without her."

— John Ruskin

APPENDIX

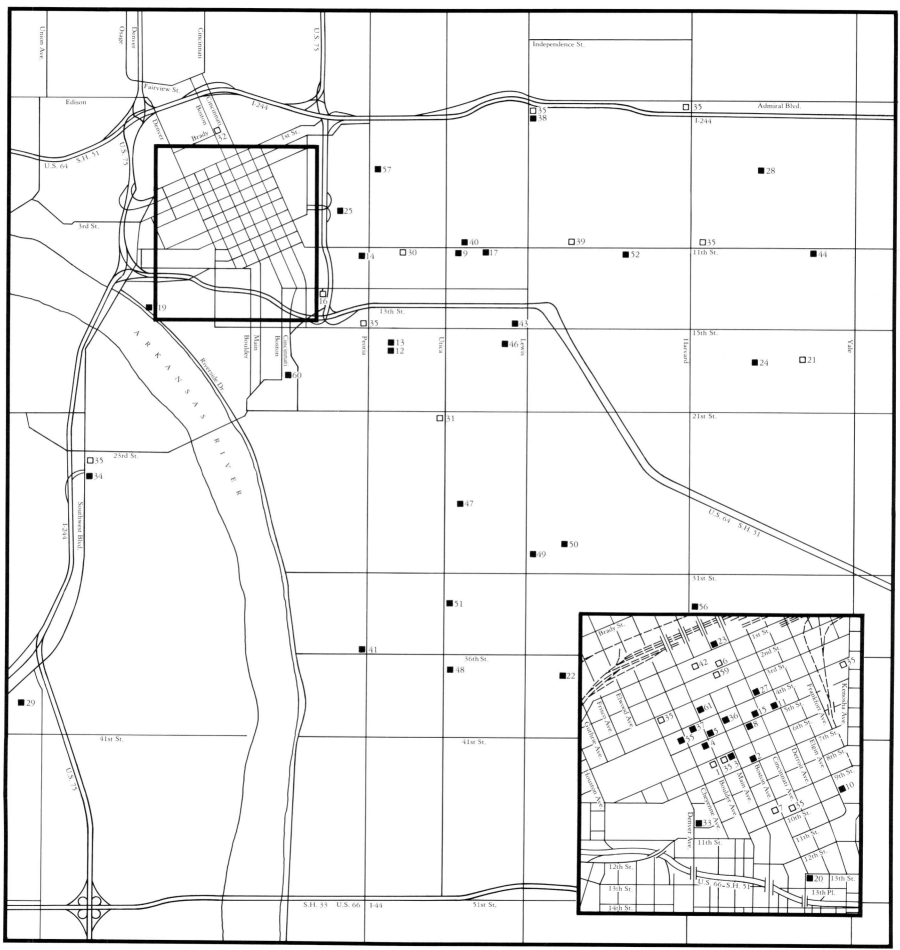

ART DECO ARCHITECTURE / TULSA, OKLAHOMA

Map figures are followed by the building name and date built, location, and architect or designer.

ZIGZAG

1. Medical and Dental Arts Bldg. (1927)
   108 West 6th Street
   Arthur M. Atkinson
   Joseph R. Koberling, Jr.
   Demolished July 1970

2. Oklahoma Natural Gas (1928)
   624 South Boston Avenue
   Arthur M. Atkinson
   Frederick V. Kershner

3. Public Service of Oklahoma (1929)
   (Transok Pipeline)
   600 South Main Street
   Arthur M. Atkinson
   Joseph R. Koberling, Jr.

4. Halliburton-Abbott (1929)
   (Sears/Skaggs)
   500 South Boulder Avenue
   Frank C. Walter
   Demolished 1980

5. Gillette-Tyrrell (1930)
   (Pythian)
   423 South Boulder Avenue
   Edward W. Saunders

6. Bliss Hotel (1929)
   123 South Boston Avenue
   L. I. Shumway
   Demolished February 1973

7. Genet Building (1930)
   (American Airlines Bldg.)
   914 South Boston Avenue
   Noble Fleming
   Joseph R. Koberling, Jr.
   Demolished April, 1969

8. Philcade (1930)
   (Stanolind/Amoco)
   511 South Boston Avenue
   Smith & Senter
   Leon B. Senter

9. Milady's Cleaners (ca. 1930)
   (La Maison)
   1736-38 East 11th Street

10. Warehouse Market (1929)
    925 South Elgin Avenue
    B. Gaylord Noftsger

11. Southwestern Bell Main Dial Bldg.
    (1924, 1930)
    424 South Detroit Avenue
    I. R. Timlin

12. Christ the King Church (1926)
    1530 South Rockford Avenue
    Byrne & Ryan
    Francis Barry Byrne

13. Marquette School (1932)
    1519 South Quincy Avenue
    F. W. Redlich

14. Adah Robinson Residence (1927)
    1119 South Owasso Avenue
    Bruce Goff

15. Tulsa Club (1927)
    115 East 5th Street
    Rush, Endacott & Rush
    Bruce Goff

16. Page Warehouse (1927)
    408 East 13th Street
    Rush, Endacott & Rush
    Bruce Goff
    Demolished November 1977

17. Guaranty Laundry (1928)
    (Page Van Lines)
    2036 East 11th Street
    Rush, Endacott & Rush
    Bruce Goff

18. Midwest Equitable Meter (1929)
    3130 Charles Page Boulevard
    Rush, Endacott & Goff
    Bruce Goff

19. Riverside Studio (1929)
    (Spotlight Theatre)
    1381 Riverside Drive
    Rush, Endacott & Goff
    Bruce Goff

20. Boston Avenue Methodist Church
    (1929)
    1301 South Boston Avenue
    Rush, Endacott & Rush
    Bruce Goff, Adah M. Robinson

21. Merchant's Exhibit Building (1930)
    Tulsa State Fairgrounds
    Endacott & Goff
    Bruce Goff

22. Richard Lloyd Jones Residence
    "Westhope" (1929)
    3704 South Birmingham Avenue
    Frank Lloyd Wright

PWA

23. Tulsa Union Depot (1931)
    3 South Boston Avenue
    R. C. Stephens

24. Fairgrounds Pavilion (1932)
    Tulsa State Fairgrounds
    L. I. Shumway

25. Tulsa Fire Alarm Building (1931)
    1010 East 8th Street
    Smith & Senter
    Frederick V. Kershner

26. Tulsa Municipal Airport
    Administration Building (1932)
    6600 East Apache Avenue
    Smith & Senter
    Frederick V. Kershner
    Demolished 1969

27. Union Bus Depot (1935)
    319 South Cincinnati Avenue
    Leon B. Senter & Associates
    Frederick V. Kershner

28. Will Rogers High School (1938)
    3909 East 5th Place
    Arthur M. Atkinson
    Leon B. Senter and
    Joseph R. Koberling, Jr.

29. Daniel Webster High School (1938)
    1919 West 40th Street
    Arthur M. Atkinson
    John Duncan Forsyth, William H.
    Wolaver and Raymond Kerr

STREAMLINE

30. Cities Service Oil Co. Station
    (ca. 1933)
    1502 East 11th Street
    M. R. Pettingill

31. Mid Continent Oil Co. Station
    Sapulpa, Oklahoma (Vitrolite) (1929)
    2102 South Utica (Porcelain) (1931)
    Donald McCormick

32. Marathon Oil Co. Station (1931)
    201 North Boston Avenue

33. Skelly Oil Co. Station (1938)
    (Homer's Downtown Gulf)
    829 South Denver Avenue

34. Texas Oil Co. Service Station (1936)
    2501 Southwest Boulevard
    Walter Dorwin Teague

35. Silver Castle Restaurants (1936-40)
    15th & Peoria
    Admiral & Lewis
    6th & Main
    113 East 10th
    4th & Kenosha
    11th & Indianapolis
    3rd & Denver
    5600 East 11th
    2341 South Quannah
    3240 East Admiral Place
    Ora Overholzer

36. Lerner Shop (remodeled ca. 1931)
    419 South Main Street

37. Security Federal (remodeled 1937)
    (Court of Three Sisters)
    120 West 4th Street
    Harry H. Mahler

38. People's State Bank (remodeled 1941)
    2408 East Admiral Boulevard

39. Whitlock's Grocery (1937)
    2623 East 11th Street

40. Tulsa Monument Company (1936)
    1735 East 11th Street
    Harry H. Mahler

41. City Veterinary Clinic (1942)
    3550 South Peoria Avenue
    Joseph R. Koberling, Jr.

42. Palace Theater (remodeled 1935)
    118 South Main Street
    Joseph R. Koberling, Jr.
    Demolished 1973

43. Delman Theater (1938)
    2335 East 15th Street
    W. Scott Dunne

44. Will Rogers Theater (1941)
    4502 East 11th Street
    Jack Corgan and W. J. Moore

45. KVOO Transmitter Station (1932)
    15050 East 11th Street
    John T. Blair

46. J. B. McGay Residence (1936)
    1551 South Yorktown Place
    Joseph R. Koberling, Jr.

47. T. N. Law Residence (1935)
    1841 East 27th Street
    William H. Wolaver

48. Arnold Ungerman Residence (1941)
    1718 East 37th Street
    Leo Clark

49. Burtner N. Fleeger Residence (1937)
    2424 East 29th Street
    Frederick V. Kershner

50. John Duncan Forsyth Residence
    (1937)
    2827 South Birmingham Place
    John Duncan Forsyth
    Robert E. West

51. Jesse D. Davis Residence (1936)
    3231 South Utica Avenue
    Frances Davis

52. William D. Whenthoff Residence
    (1935)
    1142 South College Avenue

53. John Leroy Shakley Residence (1937)
    7219 South Evanston Avenue

54. Howard J. Sherman Residence (1937)
    7228 South Evanston Avenue

55. Mayo Motor Inn (1950)
    416 South Cheyenne Avenue
    Leon B. Senter & Associates

56. Morrow Geophysical Building (1948)
    (American Red Cross Bldg.)
    3345 South Harvard Avenue

57. Midwest Marble and Tile (1945)
    (Type Service Corp.)
    507 South Quaker Avenue
    Robert E. West

58. Century Geophysical Corp. (1946)
    6650 East Apache Avenue
    Frederick V. Kershner

59. Parkcade Parking Garage (1949)
    2nd Street & Boston Avenue
    Henry R. Lohman Const. Co.
    Demolished 1973

60. Phoenix Cleaners (1947)
    125 East 18th Street

61. Newspaper Printing Corp. Office
    (1947)
    317 South Boulder Avenue
    John Cushing

THE ARCHITECTURAL PROFESSION 1925-1940

The inclusion of the following material was prompted by the difficulty which we encountered in locating biographical information on the architects of the Art Deco buildings. With few exceptions, we could find little or no information on our local architects in traditional sources. Much of our information was eventually gathered through numerous oral interviews. Because these sources stood in danger of being lost to us we decided to extend our research to include all those architects practicing in Tulsa in the Art Deco era.

The following biographical sketches are of those Tulsans who were licensed to practice architecture in Oklahoma 1925-1940, following the enactment of the licensing law in 1925. Several reknowned architects who came to Tulsa for a commissioned work are also included: F. Barry Byrne, Edward B. Delk, Arthur S. Keene, Leslie B. Simpson, and Frank Lloyd Wright.

Only a few of the forty-eight architects listed here designed Deco structures but because they practiced at the same time in the same locality their work and their interrelationships afford a fuller understanding of the era.

As the first published material on many of Tulsa's early architects we hope that this will serve as a starting place for further research of their contributions to Tulsa's history and to our cityscape.

Buildings included here are representative of the architect's work and, where possible, both commercial and residential buildings are listed. Buildings are in chronological order and with the exception of schools, are located by position on the block. Locations of schools and residences are by street number. All residences are referred to by the name of the original owner.

Unless otherwise noted, all locations of partnerships and buildings are Tulsa, Oklahoma. The symbol (▼) preceeding a building indicates that it is no longer standing.

1. ARTHUR M. ATKINSON, A.I.A.
(1891-1949)

Born: Kansas City, Missouri
Training: Apprenticeship
Oklahoma License: 1925-1949
Tulsa Practice: 1916-1949

PARTNERSHIPS

Schumaker, Atkinson & Olston, 1920-1921
  (William A. Schumaker, Frank Olston)
Atkinson & Olston, 1921-1924
Atkinson & Murray, 1948-1949
  (David G. Murray)

BUILDINGS

Thompson Building, southwest corner of
  5th & Boston (1921, Atkinson & Olston)
Vandever Dry Goods Store, east side of
  5th Street between Boston and Main
  (1924, Atkinson & Olston)
▼ Seidenbach Store, east side of Main
  between 3rd and 4th (1926)
▼ Medical and Dental Arts Building,
  southwest corner 6th and Boulder (1927)
Oklahoma Natural Gas Building,
  northwest corner 7th and Boston (1928)
▼ Court Arcade Building, northwest corner
  6th and Boulder (1928)
Public Service Company Building (Transok
  Pipeline Company Building), southwest
  corner 6th and Main (1929)
National Guard Armory, Tulsa State
  Fairgrounds (1941)
Lorton Hall, Tulsa University (1948)

A. M. Atkinson became a registered professional engineer when the registration law went into effect in Oklahoma in 1935.

2. ROSS B. BAZE
(1903-   )

Born: Tulsa, Indian Territory
Training: University of California at
  Berkley, B.A. Architecture, 1926
Oklahoma License: 1927-1942
Tulsa Practice: 1927-1942

PARTNERSHIPS

Popkin & Baze, 1927-1929
  (Charles A. Popkin)

BUILDINGS

Lee Clinton Building, southwest corner
  5th and Cheyenne (1927)
Lon Stansbury Residence, 325 North
  Madison
Dr. Jim Perry Residence, 3131 South
  Zunis

Baze currently resides in New Orleans, Louisiana.

3. J. LELAND BENSON, A.I.A.
(1889-1975)

Born: Nevada, Missouri
Training: University of Kansas, Lawrence,
  Kansas, Architectural Engineering
Oklahoma License: 1937-1942
Tulsa Practice: 1938-1940

PARTNERSHIPS

None

BUILDINGS

Franklin Bernsen Residence, 2819
  South Cincinnati

Benson designed a plaque for Adah Robinson in Owen park. He was a draftsman for John Duncan Forsyth and worked on Ardmore Air Force Base, Ardmore, Oklahoma, 1941.

4. RALPH M. BLACK, A.I.A.
(1883-1976)

Born: Rich Hill, Missouri
Training: Attended Washington
  University, St. Louis, Missouri
Oklahoma License: 1925-1976
Tulsa Practice: 1914-1972

PARTNERSHIPS

A. W. Black & Son, 1914-1925
  (A. W. Black)
Black & West, 1945-1965 (Robert E. West)
Black, West & Wozencraft, 1965-1972
  (Wallace O. Wozencraft)

BUILDINGS

Gallais Building (Kennedy Building on
  4th Street side), northeast corner 4th
  and Boston (1916)
▼ Springer Clinic, southwest corner 6th
  and Cincinnati (1918)
Spartan Aircraft, Tulsa International
  Airport (1941).
Tulsa County Courthouse, Civic Center
  (1953, Black & West)
Skelly Oil Building, northeast corner 15th
  and Main (1959, Black & West)
Post Office & Federal Building, northwest
  corner 4th and Denver (1961, Black
  & West, Donald McCormick, Leon B.
  Senter, Associated Architects)
Pan American Building (Amoco), northeast
  corner 6th and Boston (1965, Black,
  West & Wozencraft)
Edison High School, 2906 East 41st
  Street (1957, Black & West)
McLain High School, 4929 North Peoria,
  (1959, Black & West)
Memorial High School, 5840 South
  Hudson Avenue (1962, Black & West)
Woodlawn Apartments, 216 West 19th
  Street (1923)

In the late 1930's, Black did additions to Burroughs, Lowell and Sequoyah schools.

5. JOHN THOMAS BLAIR, A.I.A.
(1885-1976)

Born: Ozark, Missouri
Training: Self Educated
Oklahoma License: 1926
Tulsa Practice: 1910-1937

PARTNERSHIPS

Blair Brothers, 1910-1926
  (Joseph E. Blair)
Blair & Calderwood, ca. 1932
  (William Calderwood)

BUILDINGS

KVOO Transmitter Station, 15050 East
  11th Street (1932)
J. Flanagan Residence, 2202 South
  Madison
J. Duffy Residence, 1131 East 21st Place
W. G. Skelly Residence, 2101 South
  Madison

Blair Brothers was the major construction company in Tulsa until the Depression. John T. Blair, Charles Evans and Fred Knoblock did all of the design work and working drawings for Blair Brothers. They designed and built houses in Stonebreaker Heights, Maple Ridge, Sunset Terrace and Forrest Hills. The W. G. Skelly residence is on the National Register of Historic Places.

6. LAWRENCE E. BLUE, A.I.A.
(1874-1963)

Born: Chillicothe, Missouri
Training: Apprenticeship
Oklahoma License: 1925-1952
Tulsa Practice: 1910-1963

PARTNERSHIPS

Blue & Blue, 1927-1931
  (Clarence H. Blue)

BUILDINGS

Memorial Park and Chapel, southeast
  corner of 51st and Memorial (1928,
  Blue & Blue)
Tom S. Loffland Residence, 3105 South
  Peoria (Fred Knoblock and L. E. Blue,
  Associated Architects)
Cass A. Mayo Residence, 2301 South
  Boston
John D. Mayo Residence, 1401 South
  Cheyenne

Blue's later work after 1928 was related to a continuing architectural and engineering development of Memorial Park, Tulsa and Memorial Park, Oklahoma City, Oklahoma.

Harry B. Blue (1895-   ), Lawrence Blue's brother, was a designer who worked with many architects in Tulsa from 1920 to 1943. Although never licensed, he designed the Ponca City Library (1934), Ponca City, Oklahoma. He designed the terra cotta on the Bliss Hotel and the Fairgrounds Pavilion, and did many renderings for L. I. Shumway. He also did a rendering of Will Rogers High School. Blue worked for the Library of Congress on the Historic Preservation Committee. He currently resides in Portland, Oregon.

7. FRANCIS BARRY BYRNE, A.I.A.
(1883-1967)

Born: Chicago, Illinois
Training: Apprenticed to Frank Lloyd
Wright, 1902-1907

PARTNERSHIPS

Byrne & Willitson, ca. 1910, Seattle,
Washington (Andrew Willitson)
Associate of Walter Burley Griffin,
1914-1916, Chicago, Illinois
Byrne & Ryan, ca. 1920, Chicago, Illinois
(John Ryan)

BUILDINGS

Church of St. Thomas The Apostle,
Chicago, Illinois (1923-1924)
St. Patrick's Church, Racine, Wisconsin
(1923-1924)
Christ The King Church, 1530 South
Rockford Avenue, Tulsa, Oklahoma
(1926)
Church of Christ The King, Cork,
Ireland (1928-1929)
St. Columbia Church, St. Paul, Minnesota
(1948)
St. Francis Xavier, Kansas City, Missouri
(1948)
St. Benedict's Abbey, Atchison, Kansas
(1955)
St. Francis Xavier High School, Wilmette,
Illinois (1922)

8. WILLIAM HENRY CAMERON CALDERWOOD
(1899-1974)

Born: Ireland
Training: Attended Queen's College,
Belfast, Ireland
Attended University of California at
Los Angeles, Los Angeles, California
Oklahoma License: 1929-1971
Tulsa Practice: 1929-1971

PARTNERSHIPS

Blair & Calderwood, ca. 1932
(John T. Blair)

BUILDINGS

Brook Theater, southeast corner 34th and
Peoria (1949)
Brookside Professional Building, southeast
corner 35th and Peoria (1953)
Dale Carter Residence, 2723 South
Birmingham Place

W. H. C. Calderwood designed several
residences in Bartlesville.

9. MARSHALL CANFIELD CROSS, A.I.A.
(1886-1973)

Born: Fairfax, Virginia
Training: Apprenticeship
Oklahoma License: 1925-1937
Tulsa Practice: 1921-1934

PARTNERSHIPS

Mahler & Cross, ca. 1920 (Harry Mahler)
Cross & Saunders, 1923-1924
(Edward Saunders)

Cross & Duggan, 1928-1930
(Frederick A. Duggan)

BUILDINGS

▼ Oklahoma Iron Works Office Building,
northeast corner Iroquois and Archer
(1920, Mahler & Cross)
▼ Jarecki Manufacturing Company, West 1st
between Main and Boulder (1920,
Mahler & Cross)
▼ Tulsa Business College, West Denver
between 4th and 5th (1928,
Cross & Duggan)
Lorraine Apartments, northeast corner
11th and Denver (1924)

10. EDWARD BUEHLER DELK, A.I.A.
(1885-1956)

Born: Scholarie, New York
Training: University of Pennsylvania,
Pittsburg, Pennsylvania
University of London, London,
England, Graduate Studies

PARTNERSHIPS

None

BUILDINGS

Plaza Shopping Center, Kansas City,
Missouri (1923-1924, with the J. C.
Nichols Company)
Millcreek Building, Kansas City, Missouri
(1923-1924)
Kansas City Country Club, Kansas City,
Missouri (1925)
Millcreek Viaduct, Kansas City, Missouri
(1926, Kansas City Park Board)
Villa Philmont, Cimmarron, New Mexico
(1926)
Philbrook (Philbrook Art Center) 27th
and South Rockford (1927)
Philtower Building, northeast corner 4th
and Boston (1927, Delk and Keene
& Simpson, Associated Architects)
Starlight Theater, Swope Park, Kansas
City, Missouri (1950)
Mary Hibbard Residence, 6101 Mission
Drive, Kansas City, Missouri
T. J. Madden Residence, 1001 West 57th
Street, Kansas City, Missouri
Dr. T. G. Orr Residence, 5930 Mission
Boulevard, Kansas City, Missouri

Delk practiced in Kansas City, Missouri
from 1922 to 1956. He was brought to
Oklahoma by Waite Phillips to do work for
Phillips Petroleum in Bartlesville,
Oklahoma. There Delk built a house for
Frank Phillips and several vice-presidents
of Phillips Petroleum. The Dr. T. G. Orr
residence was awarded the Gold Medal
for design from the Kansas City A.I.A.
Philbrook and the Philtower Building are
on the National Register of Historic Places.

11. FREDERICK ALEXANDER DUGGAN, A.I.A.
(1878-1955)

Born: St. Louis, Missouri
Training: Apprenticeship

Oklahoma License: 1925-1955
Tulsa Practice: 1916-1955

PARTNERSHIPS

Cross & Duggan, 1928-1930
(Marshall C. Cross)

BUILDINGS

Immanuel Baptist Church, southwest
corner 3rd and Xanthus (1926)
▼ Tulsa Business College, west side of
Denver between 4th and 5th (1928,
Cross & Duggan)
M. J. Glass Apartments, 214 South
Cheyenne (1923)
J. M. Gillette Residence, 2130 East
15th Street
A. E. Durran Residence, 2877 South
Utica
F. W. Insull Residence, 1145 East 16th
Street

Licensed in Arkansas, Illinois, Missouri
and Oklahoma, his early work was done in
St. Louis where he designed several
threaters.

12. ASBURY ENDACOTT, A.I.A.
(1887-1944)

Born: Eudora, Kansas
Training: Attended Kansas State A & M
(Kansas State University), Manhattan,
Kansas
Oklahoma License: 1925-1934
Tulsa Practice: 1913-1934

PARTNERSHIPS

Rush, Endacott & Rush, 1915-1929
(A. W. Rush, E. A. Rush)
Rush, Endacott & Goff, 1929-1930
(Bruce Goff)
Endacott & Goff, 1930-1934

BUILDINGS

Wright Building, northeast corner 3rd
and Boulder (1917, Rush, Endacott
& Rush)
Tulsa Municipal Building (Old City Hall),
southwest corner 4th and Cincinnati
(1917, Rush, Endacott & Rush)
First National Bank Building (Reunion
Center), northeast corner 4th and
Main (1919, Rush, Endacott & Rush)
Atlas Life Building, east side of Boston
between 4th and 5th (1922, Rush,
Endacott & Rush)
Tulsa Club Building, northwest corner
5th and Cincinnati (1927, Rush,
Endacott & Rush)
▼ Page Warehouse, southeast corner 13th
and Elgin (1927, Rush, Endacott
& Rush)
Guaranty Laundry, southeast corner 11th
and South Xanthus Place (1928, Rush,
Endacott & Rush)
Boston Avenue Methodist Church, 13th
and Boston (1929, Rush, Endacott
& Rush)
Riverside Studio (Spotlight Theater),
northeast corner 14th and Riverside
Drive (1929, Rush, Endacott & Goff)

Midwest Equitable Meter Company
(Natco Building #4), 3130 Charles
Page Boulevard (1929, Rush, Endacott
& Goff)
▼ Merchant's Exhibit Building, Tulsa State
Fairgrounds (1930, Endacott & Goff)

Endacott was a structural engineer and
served on the State Architectural Board
(1925-1936). He designed the water and
sewer plants at Mohawk Park. He did the
original structural drawings for the tower
at Boston Avenue Methodist Church.
Endacott had a major part in the structural
design of the old Skelly Building, Chamber
of Commerce Building and the Standard
Parts Building. The Tulsa Municipal
Building and the First National Bank
Building (Reunion Center) are on the
National Register of Historic Places.

13. ALFRED CLAIRE "FRENCHIE" FABRY
(1885-1970)

Born: Alsace-Lorraine, France
Training: Attended Ecole Des Beaux Arts,
Paris, France
Attended Boston Institute of Technology
Oklahoma License: 1944-1963
Tulsa Practice: 1911-1963

PARTNERSHIPS

Fleming & Fabry, 1928-1929
(Noble B. Fleming)

BUILDINGS

Mincks Hotel (Adams Hotel), southeast
corner 4th and Cheyenne (1928)

14. NOBLE B. FLEMING
(1892-1937)

Born: Oklahoma City, Indian Territory
Training: Apprenticed to Hook & Park,
Oklahoma City, Oklahoma
Oklahoma License: 1925-1937
Tulsa Practice: 1919-1937

PARTNERSHIPS

Thompson & Fleming, 1919-1921
(J. C. Thompson)
Fleming & Fabry, 1928-1929 (A. C. Fabry)
Fleming & Koberling, 1933-1937
(J. R. Koberling, Jr.)

BUILDINGS

Tri-State Building (Silvey Building), east
side of Main between 6th & 7th (1927)
Thomas Cadillac Building (L & M Office
Supply) southwest corner 10th and
Boston (1928)
▼ Genet Building (American Airlines
Building) west side Boston between
9th and 10th (1930)
Vinita City Hall, Vinita, Oklahoma (1935)
Blue Jacket High School, Blue Jacket,
Oklahoma (1935, remodel, Fleming
& Koberling)
Richard Travis Residence (Tulsa Garden
Center) 2435 South Peoria (1918)
O. C. Lassiter Residence, 1586 Swan Drive

After the Depression hit Tulsa in 1930, Fleming and Koberling's practice consisted largely of WPA work on schools, city halls and other government contracts.

15. JOHN DUNCAN FORSYTH, A.I.A.
(1886-1963)

Born: Florence, Italy
Training: Attended Edinburgh College, Scotland
Sorbonne, Paris, France
Oklahoma License: 1925-1963
Tulsa Practice: 1925-1963

PARTNERSHIPS
None

BUILDINGS

Marland Mansion, Ponca City, Oklahoma (1926)
Southern Hills Country Club, southeast corner 61st and Lewis (1936, J. D. Forsyth and D. McCormick, Associated Architects)
Will Rogers Memorial, Claremore, Oklahoma (1938)
Pensacola Dam on Grand River, Mayes County, Oklahoma (1938)
All Souls Unitarian Church, northwest corner 30th and Peoria (1957)
Webster High School, 1919 West 40th Street (1938, J. D. Forsyth, W. Wolaver, and R. Kerr, Associated Architects; A. M. Atkinson, Supervising Architect)
R. Otis McClintock Residence, 2211 East 41st Street (J. D. Forsyth and D. McCormick, Associated Architects)
B. B. Blair Residence, 2800 South Boston
J. E. Mabee Residence, 2121 East 30th Street
John C. Mullins Residence, 2105 Forrest Boulevard
Howard Whitehill Residence, 7157 South Evanston

16. WILLIAM ALVA FRY, A.I.A.
(1889-1965)

Born: Grandin, Missouri
Training: International Correspondence Schools, Scranton, Pennsylvania (Architectural Engineering), 1908
Oklahoma License: 1947-1964
Tulsa Practice: 1920-1965

PARTNERSHIPS
None

BUILDINGS

Gavin Apartments, southwest corner 8th and Cheyenne (1922)
Barry Apartments, southeast corner 10th and Cincinnati (1922)
Ahlum Apartments, west side of Denver between 14th and 15th (1922)
Tulsa World Model Home, 1546 south Yorktown Place (1923)
Residences for Neil Grubb,
  1216 East 25th Street,
  1204 East 25th Street,
  1238 Hazel Boulevard,
  1143 Hazel Boulevard

Fry designed many bungalows in the Brookside area. From 1945 to 1965 he was Field Superintendent for Leon Senter & Associates.

17. BRUCE GOFF
(1904-   )

Born: Alton, Kansas
Training: Apprenticed to Rush, Endacott & Rush
Oklahoma License: 1930—
Tulsa Practice: 1915-1934

PARTNERSHIPS

Rush, Endacott & Goff, 1929-1930 (E. A. Rush, Asbury Endacott)
Endacott & Goff, 1930-1934

BUILDINGS

Tulsa Club, northwest corner 5th and Cincinnati (1927, Rush, Endacott & Rush; Bruce Goff, Designer)
▼Page Warehouse, southeast corner 13th and Elgin (1927, Rush, Endacott & Rush; Bruce Goff, Designer)
Guaranty Laundry, southeast corner 11th and South Xanthus Place (1928, Rush, Endacott & Rush; Bruce Goff, Designer)
Boston Avenue Methodist Church, 13th and Boston (1929, Rush, Endacott & Rush; Bruce Goff, Designer)
Riverside Studio (Spotlight Theater) northeast corner 14th and Riverside Drive (1929, Rush, Endacott & Goff)
Midwest Equitable Meter Company (Natco Building #4) 3130 Charles Page Boulevard (1929, Rush, Endacott & Goff)
▼Merchants Exhibit Building, Tulsa State Fairgrounds (1930, Endacott & Goff)
Seabee Chapel, Camp Park, California (1945)
Bavinger House, Norman, Oklahoma (1950)
Price Studio, Bartlesville, Oklahoma (1953)
Price Studio #2, Bartlesville, Oklahoma (1956)

Goff graduated from Central High School, Tulsa, Oklahoma in 1922. In 1934, he joined Chicago artist Alfonso Iannelli for a brief period and then taught at the Chicago Academy of Fine Arts. In 1947, Goff became a professor at the University of Oklahoma. In January of 1948, he became Chairman of the Department of Architecture and resigned December, 1955. He currently resides in Tyler, Texas.

18. ARTHUR SAMUEL KEENE, A.I.A., F.A.I.A.
(1875-1966)

Born: Boston, Massachusetts
Training: M.I.T., Cambridge, Massachusetts, B.S. Architecture, 1898
Traveled to England, France and Italy
Oklahoma License: 1925-1961

PARTNERSHIPS

Keene & Simpson, 1919-1955, Kansas City, Missouri (Leslie B. Simpson)

Keene, Simpson & Murphy, 1955-1961, Kansas City, Missouri (John T. Murphy)

BUILDINGS

Philtower Building, northeast corner 5th and Boston (1927-1928, E. B. Delk and Keene & Simpson, Associated Architects)
Scottish Rite Temple (WWII Memorial Building, Scottish Rite Temple) Kansas City, Missouri (1930, Keene & Simpson)
Jackson County Court Houses, Kansas City, Missouri and Independence, Missouri (1933, Keene & Simpson)
St. Luke's Hospital, Kansas City, Missouri (1954, Keene & Simpson)
E. J. Sweeney Residence, 5921 Ward Park Place, Kansas City, Missouri (Keene & Simpson)

Keene & Simpson were responsible for the architectural supervision of the Philtower Building. The firm was also hired on a consultant basis to ascertain the structural soundness of Boston Avenue Methodist Church. The Philtower is on the National Register of Historic Places.

19. RAYMOND KERR, A.I.A.
(1891-1943)

Born: Pendleton, Indiana
Training: Kansas State University, Manhattan, Kansas, B.A. Architecture 1917
Oklahoma License: 1925-1943
Tulsa Practice: 1925-1944

PARTNERSHIPS
None

BUILDINGS

Manual Arts School (Manual Arts Building), southwest corner 9th and Cincinnati (1922, W. H. Wolaver and R. Kerr, Associated Architects)
Webster High School, 1929 West 40th Street (1938, J. D. Forsyth, W. H. Wolaver, and R. Kerr, Associated Architects; A. M. Atkinson, Supervising Architect)
Residence, 2664 East 37th Street
Rayburn Foster Residence, Bartlesville, Oklahoma

R. Kerr designed prefabricated porcelain filling stations for major oil companies at Dressler Engineering. He designed numerous schools and residences while working for L. I. Shumway.

20. FREDERICK VANCE KERSHNER, A.I.A.
(1904-1980)

Born: McCurtain, Oklahoma, Choctaw Nation, Indian Territory
Training: Oklahoma A & M (Oklahoma State University), Stillwater, Oklahoma B. Architecture, 1926
Attended American School of Fine Arts, Fountainebleau, France
Oklahoma License: 1926-1980
Tulsa Practice: 1925-1980

PARTNERSHIPS
None

BUILDINGS

Tulsa Fire Alarm Building, southeast corner 8th & Madison (1931, Smith & Senter; F. Kershner, Designer)
▼Tulsa Municipal Airport Administration Building, northeast corner Sheridan & Apache (1931-1932, Smith & Senter; F. Kershner, Designer)
Union Bus Depot, northeast corner 4th & Cincinnati (1934-1935, Smith & Senter; F. Kershner, Designer)
Ardmore Air Force Base, Ardmore, Oklahoma (1941, J. D. Forsyth, W. H. Wolaver, and F. V. Kershner, Associated Architects)
Century Geophysical Corporation, 6650 East Apache (1946)
Coffeyville Memorial Hospital, Coffeyville, Kansas (1949)
Nelson Electric Supply Company, 526 North Main (1949)
Nimitz Junior High School, 3111 East 56th (1961)
Burtner Fleeger Residence, 2424 East 29th Street
Ira E. Sanditen Residence, 3314 East 51st

After returning from the American School of Fine Arts in France, Kershner worked for Arthur Atkinson. He next joined J. D. Forsyth's firm and worked on the Marland Mansion in Ponca City, Oklahoma. In 1928, he joined Stanley Simmons and Horace Peaslee in Washington, D.C. Returning to Tulsa, he joined the firm of Smith and Senter. In 1935, he worked briefly for Donald McCormick before starting his own firm.

21. FRED L. KNOBLOCK, A.I.A.
(1891-1969)

Born: Stillwater, Indian Territory
Training: Oklahoma A & M (O.S.U.) Stillwater, Oklahoma, A.B., 1912
Oklahoma License: 1925-1940
Tulsa Practice: 1925-1939

PARTNERSHIPS
None

BUILDINGS

T. S. Loffland Residence, 3105 South Peoria (F. L. Knoblock and Lawrence Blue, Associated Architects)
Commonwealth Company Residences:
  1132 East 20th Street,
  1234 East 24th Street,
  1247 East 24th Street,
  1231 East 21st Place,
  1228 East 21st Place,
  1223 East 21st Place

Knoblock worked for Blair Brothers, People's Home Corporation and Commonwealth Company in Tulsa. He left Tulsa in 1939 for Washington D.C. where he became Chief of the Architectural Engineering Branch of the G.S.A. and was responsible for the production of architectural specifications for all of the federal buildings erected by the G.S.A. He was associated with a group of architects who remodeled the White House during the Truman administration.

22. JOSEPH R. KOBERLING, JR., A.I.A. (1900-   )

Born: Budapest, Hungary
Training: Armour Institute, Chicago, Illinois, B.A. Architecture, 1925
Oklahoma License: 1928-
Tulsa Practice: 1925-

PARTNERSHIPS

Redlich & Koberling, 1929-1931
    (F. W. Redlich)
Fleming & Koberling 1933-1937
    (Noble B. Fleming)
Koberling & Brandborg, 1946-1956
    (Lennart Brandborg)

BUILDINGS

▼ Medical and Dental Arts Building, southwest corner 6th & Boulder (1927, A. M. Atkinson, Architect; J. R. Koberling, Designer)
▼ Genet Building (American Airlines Building) west side Boston between 9th & 10th (1930, N. Fleming, Architect; J. R. Koberling, Jr., Designer)
Public Service Company Building (Transok Pipeline Company Building) southwest corner 6th & Main (1929, A. M. Atkinson, Architect; J. R. Koberling, Designer)
▼ Palace Theater, Main between 1st & 2nd (1935, remodel)
City Veterinary Clinic, northwest corner 36th & Peoria (1942)
Chamber of Commerce Building, northeast corner 6th & Boston (1951)
Oklahoma Osteopathic Hospital, east side Jackson between 9th & 11th (1953)
Tulsa City County Library, southwest corner 4th & Denver (1956, J. R. Koberling and Charles W. Ward, Associated Architects)
Blue Jacket High School, Blue Jacket, Oklahoma (1935, remodel, Fleming & Koberling)
Will Rogers High School, 3909 East 5th Place (1938, J. R. Koberling and L. B. Senter, Associated Architects; A. M. Atkinson, Supervising Architect)
McGay Residence, 1551 South Yorktown Place
J. S. Childs Residence, 1600 South Madison
Tribune House of Progress, 2131 East 21st Street

Koberling currently resides in Tulsa, Oklahoma.

23. O. "OTTO" KUBATZKY (1869-1960)

Born: Frankfort, Germany
Training: University of Frankfort, Frankfort, Germany
Oklahoma License: 1925-1933
Tulsa Practice: 1922-1932

PARTNERSHIPS

None

BUILDINGS

Alhambra Square & Theater, northeast corner 15th & Peoria (1925)
Residence, 303 East 29th Street

In 1890 Kubatzky immigrated to St. Louis. He practiced architecture there and built Mount Carmel Catholic Church and Veronica Park addition 1906-1907.

24. ALBERT JOSEPH LOVE (1880-1956)

Born: Jerseyville, Illinois
Training: Apprenticeship
Oklahoma License: 1925-1956
Tulsa Practice: 1916-1939

PARTNERSHIPS

None

BUILDINGS

Clinton Junior High School, 2224 West 41st Street (1925)
Oklahoma Military Academy (Claremore College), Claremore, Oklahoma
Administration Building, Eastern State Hospital, Vinita, Oklahoma
Whitaker State Children's Home, Pryor, Oklahoma (1950)

Love built more than 150 schools, hospitals and other structures in northeastern Oklahoma. In 1939, he left Tulsa and moved to Spavinaw, Oklahoma.

25. DONALD McCORMICK, A.I.A., F.A.I.A. (1898-   )

Born: Wilkes-Barre, Pennsylvania
Training: Cornell University, Ithaca, New York, B.A. Architecture, 1921
Oklahoma License: 1926-
Tulsa Practice: 1926-

PARTNERSHIPS

None

BUILDINGS

▼ Mid-Continent Oil Service Station — Diamond DX, Sapulpa, Oklahoma (1929)
Southern Hills Country Club, 61st & Lewis (1936, J. D. Forsyth and D. McCormick, Associated Architects)
Bureau of Mines, Bartlesville, Oklahoma (1941, D. McCormick and F. V. Kershner, Associated Architects)
Grace Lutheran Church, northwest corner 6th Place & Lewis (1951)
Federal Court Building and Post Office, Civic Center (1961, Black & West, D. McCormick, and Leon Senter & Associates, Associated Architects)
Southroads Mall, northeast corner 41st and Yale (1963, Lathrop Douglas and D. McCormick, Associated Architects)
Cascia Hall, 25th & Yorktown (1924)

Constance Eirich Residence, 2462 East 30th Street
R. Otis McClintock Residence, 2211 East 41st Street (J. D. Forsyth and D. McCormick, Associated Architects)
Gaskell Residence, 2831 East 27th Place
Brander Residence, 2219 East 45th Place
A. H. Butler, Jr. Residence, 3311 South Zunis

McCormick has custom-built over 200 residences in Tulsa. He has completed most of the major construction at Hillcrest Medical Center. He now resides in Tulsa, Oklahoma.

26. MALCOLM L. McCUNE, A.I.A. (1889-1979)

Born: Leavenworth, Kansas
Training: University of Kansas, Lawrence, Kansas, B. Architecture, 1916
Oklahoma License: 1925-1979
Tulsa Practice: 1920-1974

PARTNERSHIPS

None

BUILDINGS

Colonial Building, northeast corner 15th and Quaker (1928)
All Souls Unitarian Church (Fitzgerald's Funeral Home), southwest corner 14th and Boulder (1930)
Utica Square Shopping Center, 21st Street between Utica and Yorktown (1952)
Southland Shopping Center, southeast corner 41st and Yale (1965)
Arthur Olson Residence, 1345 East 29th Street
Fred T. Haddock Residence, 2511 East 28th Street
Walter Helmerick Residence, 3003 South Rockford Road

McCune served as architect for Philbrook Art Center renovations and additions, 1937-1968.

27. CHARLES A. MacDONALD, A.I.A. (1870-1955)

Born: Boston, Massachusetts
Training: Apprenticeship
Oklahoma License: 1925-1926
Tulsa Practice: 1909-1926

PARTNERSHIPS

Winkler & MacDonald, 1910-1915
    (George Winkler)
MacDonald & Collignon, 1918-1919
    (G. W. Collignon)

BUILDINGS

▼ Old County Courthouse, northeast corner 6th and Boulder (1910, Winkler & MacDonald)
Palace Building, (Main Mall Building), northwest corner 4th and Main (1910, Winkler & MacDonald)
Mayo Office Building, northwest corner 5th and Main (1911, Winkler & MacDonald)

First Presbyterian Church, southeast corner 7th & Boston (1911, Winkler & MacDonald)
Holy Family Cathedral, southwest corner 8th and Boulder (1914, Winkler & MacDonald and J. P. Curtin, Associated Architects)

28. JOHN V. McDONNELL, A.I.A. (1889-1926)

Born: New York City, New York
Training: Yale University, New Haven, Connecticut, 1911
Oklahoma License: 1925-1926
Tulsa Practice: 1916-1926

PARTNERSHIPS

McDonnell & Nelson, 1916-1926
    (Beverly Nelson)

BUILDINGS

Junior League Tea Room (114 East 5th Bldg.), between Boston & Cincinnati (1924, McDonnell & Nelson)
Oaks Country Club (original building) 6900 South 49th West Avenue (1924, McDonnell & Nelson)
Irish Cottage, 1217 East 21st (McDonnell & Nelson)
Cleary Residence, 1224 East 19th Street (McDonnell & Nelson)
W. W. Heard Residence, 1325 East 31st Street (McDonnell & Nelson)
Joe Washington Residence, 1225 East 25th (McDonnell & Nelson)
Clark Rainey Residence, 2718 Riverside Drive (McDonnell & Nelson)
Greg Morton Residence, 2161 South Owasso (McDonnell & Nelson)

29. HARRY HAMILTON MAHLER (1876-1975)

Born: Chicago, Illinois
Training: Attended University of Michigan, Ann Arbor, Michigan
Oklahoma License: 1925-1952
Tulsa Practice: 1918-1939

PARTNERSHIPS

Mahler & Cross, ca. 1920 (Marshall C. Cross)

BUILDINGS

▼ Oklahoma Iron Works Office Building, northeast corner Iroquois and Archer (1920, Mahler & Cross)
▼ Jarecki Manufacturing Company, West 1st between Main and Boulder (1920, Mahler & Cross)
Masonic Temple, southwest corner 7th and Boston (1922)
Second Church of Christ Scientist, northeast corner Terrace Drive and 15th Street (1929)
Tulsa Monument Company, northwest corner 11th and Victor (1936)
Security Federal Savings and Loan, (Court of Three Sisters), 4th Street between Boulder and Cheyenne (1937, remodeled)

John Larkin Residence, 1524 South Denver
F. P. Walter Residence, 1830 South
Cheyenne

Architect and engineer, Mahler worked in
Chicago from 1898 to 1918 for the firm
of Holabird & Roche. During World War
II, he left Tulsa to build training camps in
Texas with the firm of Wyatt C. Hedrick
in Ft. Worth, Texas.

30. BEVERLY NELSON
(1891-1954)

Born: Salem, Virginia
Training: Apprenticeship
Oklahoma License: 1925-1926
Tulsa Practice: 1916-1926

PARTNERSHIPS

McDonnell & Nelson, 1916-1926
(John V. McDonnell)

BUILDINGS

Junior League Tea Room (114 East 5th
Bldg.), between Boston and Cincinnati
(1924, McDonnell & Nelson)
▼ Pierce Pennant Gas Station and Hotel,
south side 11th between Garnett and
129th East Avenue (1926)
Irish Cottage, 1217 East 21st (McDonnell
& Nelson)
Cleary Residence, 1224 East 19th
(McDonnell & Nelson)
W. W. Heard Residence, 1325 East 31st
(McDonnell & Nelson)
Joe Washington Residence, 1225 East
25th (McDonnell & Nelson)
Clark Rainey Residence, 2718 Riverside
Drive (McDonnell & Nelson)
Greg Morton Residence, 2161 South
Owasso (McDonnell & Nelson)

During and after WWII, Nelson was the
Official State Department Architect in
charge of all American buildings in
Europe.

31. FRANK MICHAEL OLSTON
(1892-1963)

Born: Sisterville, West Virginia
Training: Attended Notre Dame, Notre
Dame, Indiana
University of Pennsylvania, Philadelphia,
Pennsylvania, B.A. 1914
Oklahoma License: 1935-1959
Tulsa Practice: 1920-1959

PARTNERSHIPS

Schumaker, Atkinson & Olston, 1920-1921
(William A. Schumaker, Arthur M.
Atkinson)
Atkinson & Olston, 1921-1924

BUILDINGS

Thompson Building, southwest corner
5th and Boston (1921, Atkinson
& Olston)
Vandever Dry Goods Company, east side
of 5th Street between Boston and Main
(1924, Atkinson & Olston)

Holmes Elementary School, 1202 East
45th Place (1950)
Clinton Elementary School, 1740 North
Harvard (1953)
W. K. Warren Residence, 2435 East
28th Street
J. R. Simpson Residence, 1217 Hazel
Boulevard

F. M. Olston built Catholic Churches in
Norman, Cushing, and Ponca City,
Oklahoma. He was consulting architect
on St. Francis Hospital, Tulsa, Oklahoma.

32. CHARLES A. POPKIN
(1881-1960)

Training: Union College
Oklahoma License: 1925-1942
Tulsa Practice: 1927-1930

PARTNERSHIPS

Popkin & Baze, 1927-1929 (Ross B. Baze)

BUILDINGS

Earl Berryhill Building, Sapulpa,
Oklahoma
Creek County Court House, Sapulpa,
Oklahoma
▼ Sapulpa High School, Sapulpa, Oklahoma

Charles A. Popkin moved to Oklahoma
ca. 1916 and began his practice in Sapulpa.
During the Depression, he went to work
for the Bureau of Indian Affairs in
Muskogee, Oklahoma.

33. FREDERICK WILHELM "FRITZ" REDLICH, A.I.A.
(1880-1950)

Born: Mannheim, Germany
Training: University of Mannheim,
Mannheim, Germany
Oklahoma License: 1925-1931
Tulsa Practice: 1929-1931

PARTNERSHIPS

Redlich & Koberling, 1929-1931
(Joseph R. Koberling, Jr.)

BUILDINGS

Morningside Hospital (Hillcrest Hospital)
(1927)
School of Architecture Building, Oklahoma
A & M (O.S.U.) Stillwater, Oklahoma
(1918)
Monte Cassino School, 2206 South Lewis
(1928)
Marquette School, 1519 South Quincy
(1932)

Established Architecture Department at
Oklahoma A & M (O.S.U.) in 1911. He
served as Chairman until 1927 when he
resigned to take up a large private practice.
He was also a member of the first licensing
board of architects in Oklahoma.

34. JOHN WESLEY ROBB, A.I.A.
(1880-1964)

Born: Kenmundy, Illinois
Training: Apprenticeship

Oklahoma License: 1925-1962
Tulsa Practice: 1922-1962

PARTNERSHIPS

None

BUILDINGS

Stanley's Funeral Home, northeast corner
12th and Boulder (1925)
Commercial Building, west side of Main
between 6th and 7th (1927)
Stanley's Funeral Home, northwest corner
31st and Pittsburg

35. LYMAN HOWLAND RUGGLES
(1868-1954)

Born: Hancock, Michigan
Training: Apprenticeship
Oklahoma License: 1925-1942
Tulsa Practice: 1905-1954

PARTNERSHIPS

None

BUILDINGS

▼ West Tulsa State Bank, (Southwest
Building), 17th Street and Quannah
(1942)
▼ Crosby Residence, 1437 South Boulder
▼ Dr. Fred Clinton Residence, 510 South
Cheyenne

Ruggles was the second architect in Indian
Territory. He made plans for over 56
banks in small towns throughout
Oklahoma.

36. ARTHUR "E. A." RUSH
(1860-1948)

Born: Rush County, Indiana
Training: Apprenticeship
Oklahoma License: 1925-1943
Tulsa Practice: 1912-1948

PARTNERSHIPS

A. W. & E. A. Rush, 1889, Grand
Rapids, Michigan (Arthur W. Rush)
A. W. Rush & E. A. Rush, 1910, Chicago,
Illinois
E. A. Rush & Company, 1912-1915
Rush, Endacott & Rush, 1915-1929
(Asbury Endacott)
Rush, Endacott & Goff, 1929-1930
(Bruce Goff)

BUILDINGS

▼ Burleson Sanitarium, Grand Rapids,
Michigan (1885)
▼ Pythian Temple, Grand Rapids, Michigan
(ca. 1889, A. W. & E. A. Rush)
▼ Grand Rapids Chair Company, Grand
Rapids, Michigan (1890)
Wright Building, northeast corner 3rd
and Boulder (1917, Rush, Endacott
& Rush)
Tulsa Municipal Building (Old City Hall)
southwest corner 4th and Cincinnati
(1917, Rush, Endacott & Rush)
First National Bank Building (Reunion
Center), northeast corner 4th and Main
(1919, Rush, Endacott & Rush)

Atlas Life Building, east side Boston
between 4th and 5th (1922)
▼ Page Warehouse, southeast corner 13th
and Elgin (1927, Rush, Endacott &
Rush)
Tulsa Club, northwest corner 5th and
Cincinnati (1927, Rush, Endacott &
Rush)
Boston Avenue Methodist Church, 13th
and Boston (1929, Rush, Endacott &
Rush)
Vandever Residence, 3041 South Peoria
(Rush, Endacott & Rush)
H. O. McClure Residence, 1120 South
Cheyenne (Rush, Endacott & Rush)

E. A. Rush's father, A. W. Rush, was never
licensed in Oklahoma. He retired from the
firm in 1913 and died in 1923, but his
name remained in the firm until 1929.
First National Bank Building (Reunion
Center) and the Tulsa Municipal Building
are on the National Register of Historic
Places.

37. EDWARD WATKINS SAUNDERS
(1878-1964)

Born: Troy, Ohio
Training: Attended University of
Pennsylvania, Philadelphia, Pennsylvania
1910-1912
Oklahoma License: 1925-1964
Tulsa Practice: 1919-1964

PARTNERSHIPS

Butler & Saunders, 1920-1921
(Cortland L. Butler)
Cross & Saunders, 1923-1924
(M. C. Cross)

BUILDINGS

▼ Ritz Building, northeast corner 4th and
Boulder (1925)
▼ Morris Plan Bank, northwest corner 4th
and Boulder (1928)
Gillette-Tyrrell Building (Pythian)
northeast corner 5th and Boulder (1930)
Ralph Talbot Residence, 1030 East 19th
Street
Carl W. Gillette Residence, 1554 South
Yorktown Place
P. M. Kerr Residence, 1312 South Guthrie

Saunders served as a city building inspector
from 1949 to 1956.

38. LEON BISHOP SENTER, A.I.A., F.A.I.A.
(1889-1965)

Born: Morris, Johnson County, Kansas
Training: International Correspondence
Schools, Scranton, Pennsylvania,
1910 (Architectural Engineering)
Oklahoma License: 1925-1965
Tulsa Practice: 1928-1965

PARTNERSHIPS

Smith, Rea, Lovitt & Senter, 1918-1924,
Okmulgee, Oklahoma (Charles A.
Smith, Frank S. Rea, Walter Y. Lovitt)
Smith & Senter, 1924-1928, Okmulgee,
Oklahoma

Smith & Senter, 1928-1933
Senter & Associates, 1933-1965

BUILDINGS

Orpheum Theater, Okmulgee, Oklahoma (1919)

Commerce Building, Okmulgee, Oklahoma (1921)

Carnegie Public Library, Okmulgee, Oklahoma (1922)

▼ The Coliseum, west side Elgin between 5th & 6th Street (1928) (1928)

Philcade (Stanolind Building, Amoco) southeast corner 5th and Boston (1930)

University of Tulsa Stadium (Skelly Stadium) (1930)

Tulsa Fire Alarm Building, southeast corner 8th and Madison (1931)

▼ Tulsa Municipal Airport Administration Building, northeast corner Sheridan and Apache (1932, Smith & Senter) Senter)

Union Bus Depot, northeast corner 4th and Cincinnati (1935)

Service Pipe Line Building (Atlantic Richfield Building) northwest corner 6th and Cincinnati (1946)

St. John's Hospital, northeast corner 21st and Utica (1946 and 1956 Additions)

Will Rogers High School, 3909 East 5th Place (1938, J. R. Koberling and L. B. Senter, Associated Architects; A. M. Atkinson, Supervising Architect)

Booker T. Washington High School, 1631 East Woodrow Place (1950)

From 1912 to 1918 Smith, Rea & Lovitt were in Kansas City, Missouri. Senter was regarded as the Dean of Oklahoma Architects. Senter was issued License #1 when the licensing law went into effect in Oklahoma in 1925. He was the President of the State Board of Governors of Licensed Architects in Oklahoma and a charter member and past president of Oklahoma Chapter of A.I.A. Tulsa architects who first worked in Senter's office included F. V. Kershner, J. Koberling, and W. Wolaver. The Philcade is on the National Register of Historic Places.

39. LELAND I. SHUMWAY, A.I.A.
1891-1969

Born: New York City, New York
Training: Apprenticed to George Winkler
Oklahoma License: 1925-1957
Tulsa Practice: 1908-1935

PARTNERSHIPS

None

BUILDINGS

▼ Tulsa Hotel, northwest corner 3rd and Cincinnati (1912)

▼ Alexander Building, west side of Main between 3rd and 4th (1922)

▼ Albany Hotel, west side of Cheyenne between 5th and 6th (1925)

▼ Bliss Hotel, northeast corner 2nd and Boston (1929)

Fairgrounds Pavilion, Tulsa State Fairgrounds (1932)

Barnard Elementary School, 2324 East 17th Street (1925)

Lanier Elementary School, 1727 South Harvard Avenue (1925)

Roosevelt Elementary School, 1202 West Easton Street (1926)

Wilson Junior High School, 1127 South Columbia Avenue (1926)

Franklin Elementary School, 1135 South Yale Avenue (1927)

Shumway served as an architect for the Tulsa Board of Education in the 1920's and 1930's. He designed over 13 schools in Tulsa during that time.

40. LESLIE B. SIMPSON, A.I.A.
(1885-1961)

Born: Calhoun, Missouri
Training: Studied architectural correspondence courses (Calhoun, Missouri) Apprenticed to Henry Hoit, Kansas City, Missouri

PARTNERSHIPS

Keene & Simpson, 1919-1955, Kansas City, Missouri (Arthur S. Keene)
Keene, Simpson & Murphy, 1955-1961 (John T. Murphy)

BUILDINGS

Philtower Building, northeast corner 5th and Boston (1927-1928, Keene & Simpson and E. B. Delk, Associated Architects)

Scottish Rite Temple (WWII Memorial Building) Kansas City, Missouri (1930, Keene & Simpson)

Jackson County Court Houses, Kansas City, Missouri and Independence, Missouri (1933, Keene & Simpson)

E. J. Sweeney Residence, 5921 Ward Park Place, Kansas City, Missouri (Keene & Simpson)

Simpson was licensed in Missouri. The Philtower is on the National Register of Historic Places.

41. ERICH W. SIPPEL
(1877-1947)

Born: Berlin, Germany
Training: University of Berlin, Berlin, Germany, 1900
Oklahoma License: 1926-1947
Tulsa Practice: 1926-1947

PARTNERSHIPS

None

BUILDINGS

McBirney Building (Parker Building), southeast corner of 3rd and Main (1927)

Sippel was an associate of Wright & Wright in Kansas City and came to Tulsa as the firm's representative to supervise the construction of St. John's Hospital. As a member of Wright & Wright, he worked on the J. H. McBirney residence and the

Sam McBirney residence and on the Bank of Commerce Building. He also supervised construction on the E. Harwell residence (Harwelden).

42. ALEXANDER THOMSON THORNE, A.I.A.
(1887-1960)

Born: Auckland, New Zealand
Training: Attended Prince Albert College, Auckland, New Zealand
Armour Institute and Chicago Technical College
Oklahoma License: 1925-1960
Tulsa Practice: 1917-1957

PARTNERSHIPS

Thorne & Tyson, 1917-1918 (Herbert Tyson)

BUILDINGS

Mohawk Park Buildings, Mohawk Park, (1930)

E. A. Markley Residence, 1906 East 37th Street

John Knox Residence, Bartlesville, Oklahoma

P. J. McIntyre Residence, Bartlesville, Oklahoma

J. S. Dewar Residence, Bartlesville, Oklahoma

Prior to his practice in Tulsa, he worked for Henry Holsman in Chicago and for Stern and Reichert in Chicago. In 1918, he developed the map and Real Estate Plats for Tulsa (Thorne Plat Book and Thorne Atlas Book). He worked on the Dennison Dam Powerhouse with the Corps of Engineers. He designed the addition to the Marland Refining Company in Ponca City, Oklahoma.

43. FRANK C. WALTER, A.I.A.
(1870-1953)

Born: Alton, Illinois
Training: Apprenticeship
Oklahoma License: 1928-1951
Tulsa Practice: 1917-1947

PARTNERSHIPS

Edwards & Walter, ca. 1910, Atlanta, Georgia

BUILDINGS

Union Terminal, Savannah, Georgia (1895)

K. C. Auto Hotel, east side of Cincinnati between 3rd and 4th (1927)

▼ Halliburton-Abbott (Skaggs Building) southwest corner 5th and Boulder (1929)

Skiatook Community Building, Skiatook, Oklahoma (1940)

▼ Mary Brockman Apartments, northwest corner 9th and Main

F. C. Walter began his practice in Columbia, South Carolina, and then moved to Atlanta where he practiced for about 20 years before moving his practice to Tulsa. Walter was city building

inspector under Mayors Flynn and Price. From 1947 to 1950, he served as Building Inspector in Augusta, Georgia.

44. CLARENCE DILLWORTH WALTERS, A.I.A.
(1896-1946)

Born: Willmington, Delaware
Training: Delaware State College, Dover, Delaware, B. Architecture
Oklahoma License: 1930-1942
Tulsa Practice: 1918-1942

PARTNERSHIPS

Turner & Walters, 1929-1933 (Morris W. Turner)
Skelly & Walters, 1939-1942 (J. A. Skelly)

BUILDINGS

Tulsa Country Club, 7th and North Union (1937, remodel)
Residence, 1524 East 26th Place
Residence, 1526 East 26th Place
Residence, 2508 South Terwilleger

C. D. Walters, primarily a residential architect, developed Terwilleger Heights and was in the forefront of building homes that were Home Loan Corporation properties.

45. ROBERT E. WEST, A.I.A.
(1904-   )

Born: Britton, Indian Territory
Training: Oklahoma A & M (O.S.U.) Norman, Oklahoma, 1926
Oklahoma License: 1926-
Tulsa Practice: 1928-1972

PARTNERSHIPS

Black & West, 1945-1965 (Ralph M. Black)
Black, West & Wozencraft, 1965-1972 (Wallace O. Wozencraft)

BUILDINGS

Midwest Marble and Tile (Type Service Corp.) northeast corner 5th and Quaker (1945)

Skelly Building, northeast corner 15th and Main (1959, Black & West)

Post Office and Federal Building, northwest corner of 4th and Denver (1961, Black & West, Donald McCormick and Leon B. Senter & Associates, Associated Architects)

Pan American Building (Amoco) northeast corner 6th and Boston (1965, Black West & Wozencraft)

Monte Cassino School, 2206 South Lewis (1928, F. W. Redlich; R. West, Designer)

Edison High School, 2906 East 41st (1957, Black & West)

McLain High School, 4929 North Peoria Avenue (1959, Black & West)

Memorial High School, 5840 South Hudson (1962, Black & West)

John Duncan Forsyth Residence, 2827 South Birmingham Place (1937, J. D. Forsyth; R. West, Designer)

From 1926 to 1928 West worked for F. W. Redlich. In 1928 he moved to Texarkana,

Texas and worked for Whitt, Seibert & Halsey. In the early 1930's he worked for Roy Place in Tucson, Arizona. He returned to Tulsa to work for J. D. Forsyth until the war. Following WWII he began his own practice with Black. He currently resides in Tulsa, Oklahoma.

46. GEORGE WINKLER, A.I.A. (1869-1962)

Born: Donegal, Pennsylvania
Training: Curry College (Pittsburg University) Pittsburg, Pennsylvania B.A., Phi Beta Kappa
Cornell University, Ithaca, New York, B. Arch.
Columbia University, New York City, New York
Oklahoma License: 1925-1953
Tulsa Practice: 1907-1925

PARTNERSHIPS

Robinson & Winkler, 1903-1907, Pittsburg and Altoona, Pennsylvania
Winkler & McDonald, 1910-1916 (Charles A. McDonald)
Schumacher & Winkler, 1926-1930, Tampa, Florida (William A. Schumacher)
Winkler & Reid, 1930-1950, Oklahoma City, Oklahoma (Guy C. Reid)

BUILDINGS

Holy Family Cathedral, southwest corner 8th and Boulder (1914, Winkler & MacDonald, and J. P. Curtin, Associated Architects)
▼ Producers National Bank Building, north side 3rd between Main and Boulder (1916, Winkler & MacDonald)
▼ Hunt Department Store Building (Brown-Duncan) southeast corner 4th and Main (1918)
Trinity Episcopal Church, southeast corner 5th and Cincinnati (1922)
Mayo Hotel, northeast corner 5th and Boulder (1925)
Gold Star Memorial Library, Oklahoma City University, Oklahoma City, Oklahoma (1946, Winkler & Reid)
Oklahoma City Public Library, Oklahoma City, Oklahoma (1950, Winkler & Reid)
Central High School (Public Service Company Building) southeast corner 6th and Cincinnati (1910)
Daniel Hunt Residence, 1030 East 18th Street
A. L. Farmer Residence, 2222 South Madison
Lee Clinton Residence, 1322 South Guthrie

The Clinton Residence is on the National Register of Historic Places.

47. WILLIAM H. WOLAVER, A.I.A. (1900-   )

Born: Lexington, Missouri
Training: Attended University of Illinois, Urbana, Illinois

Oklahoma License: 1930-1970
Tulsa Practice: 1930-1970

PARTNERSHIPS

Wolaver & Ryan, 1955 (William H. Ryan)

BUILDINGS

Manual Arts School (Manual Arts Building) southwest corner 9th and Cincinnati (1922, W. H. Wolaver and R. Kerr, Associated Architects)
Day and Night Cleaners, southwest corner 11th and Elgin (1946)
Seismograph Service Building, southwest corner 41st and Sheridan (1956)
Adams & Leonard Building, southwest corner 13th and Main (1956, Wolaver & Ryan)
B'nai Emunah Synagogue, southwest corner 17th and Peoria (1959)
Webster High School, 1919 West 40th Street (1938, J. D. Forsyth, W. H. Wolaver, and R. Kerr, Associated Architects; A. M. Atkinson, Supervising Architect)
Ardmore Air Force Base, Ardmore, Oklahoma (1941, J. D. Forsyth, W. H. Wolaver, and F. V. Kershner, Associated Architects)
Ted Law Residence, 1841 East 27th Street

From 1920 to 1921, Wolaver worked for L. I. Shumway. He worked for Smith and Senter in the Okmulgee office and in the Tulsa office from 1921 to 1936. He now resides in Portland, Oregon.

48. FRANK LLOYD WRIGHT (1869-1959)

Born: Richland Center, Wisconsin
Training: Attended University of Wisconsin, Madison, Wisconsin, 1885-1887
Worked for J. L. Silsbee, Chicago, Illinois, 1889
Worked for Louis Sullivan, Chicago, Illinois, 1889-1893

BUILDINGS

▼ Larkin Building, New York, New York (1904)
Unity Church, Oak Park, Illinois (1906)
Taliesin East, Spring Green, Wisconsin (1911)
Midway Gardens, Chicago, Illinois (1914)
Imperial Hotel, Tokyo, Japan (1916-1922)
Design St. Mark's Tower, New York, New York (1929, never built)
Johnson Wax Museum, Racine, Wisconsin (1936)
Taliesin West, Phoenix, Arizona (1938)
Solomon R. Guggenheim Museum, New York, New York (1946)
Frederick Robie House, Chicago, Illinois (1919)
Millard House, Pasadena, California (1923)
Richard Lloyd Jones Residence "Westhope," 3700 South Birmingham Avenue, Tulsa, Oklahoma (1929)

Frank Lloyd Wright began the independent practice of architecture in 1893 in Chicago, Illinois. Wright, Henry Hobson Richardson, and Louis Sullivan are the most influential American architects of the modern era. "Westhope," Richard Lloyd Jones residence, is on the National Register of Historic Places.

NOTES

ZIGZAG

1. Angie Debo, *Tulsa: from Creek Town to Oil Capital* (Norman: University of Oklahoma Press, 1943), p. 92.
2. Sharon S. Darling, *Chicago Ceramics & Glass: An Illustrated History from 1871 to 1933* (Chicago: Chicago Historical Society, 1979), p. 172.
3. Darling, p. 200.
4. "New Halliburton-Abbott Formally Open Dec. 2," *Tulsa World,* 24 November 1929, p. 1, col. 8.
5. "Empire Builds Chandeliers that Match Beauty in Tulsa's Most Awe-Inspiring Buildings," *Tulsa Spirit,* 28 August 1929, p. 5.
6. Lerona Rosamond Morris, *Oklahoma Yesterday, Today and Tomorrow* (Guthrie. Oklahoma: Cooperative Publishing Co., 1930), p. 860.
7. Untitled clipping from the *Tulsa Spirit,* 1930, in the Leon B. Senter Unpublished Scrapbooks, ca. 1920-1960, Private Collection.
8. Untitled, undated clipping from the *Tulsa World,* in the Leon B. Senter Scrapbooks.
9. Telephone interview with Ben Ball, Architect for Southwestern Bell Telephone Co., 23 January 1980.
10. Christ the King Parish, *Christ the King Church Golden Jubilee, 1928-1979* (Tulsa, 1978).
11. Telephone interview with Rev. James D. White, author of *Tulsa Catholics,* St. Barnards Parish, 26 November 1979.
12. Barry Byrne, Unpublished notes for Father Fletcher on Christ the King Church (Parish Office Scrapbook, Tulsa, Oklahoma, December 1939).
13. "Christ the King Praised in National Art Magazine," *Tulsa World,* 3 March 1940.
14. Personal interview with Joseph R. Koberling, Jr., Architect, 21 September 1979.
15. David Gilson DeLong, *The Architecture of Bruce Goff* (New York: Garland Publishing, Inc., 1977), p. 64, in footnote 108.
16. The land belonged to the School Board. The lease contained the stipulation that no alcoholic beverages were to be served on the property, and if they were, the land would revert to the School Board. Alcoholic beverages were served when prohibition ended in Oklahoma, and the School Board exercised its rights in the contract. The Tulsa Club found itself in the position of having to repurchase the property.
17. DeLong, p. 56.
18. "The Page Furniture Depository and Warehouse," *Art in Architecture* Vol. 1, June 1978, pps. 11-13.
19. "Sand Springs Steps Forward," *Tulsa Spirit,* 29 January 1930, p. 22.
20. Frank Lloyd Wright, *An Autobiography* (New York: Duell, Sloan & Pearce, 1943), p. 168.
21. DeLong, p. 62.
22. DeLong, pps. 63-64, footnote 108. The primary contract of June 26, 1926, between C. C. Cole, Chairman of the Building Committee, and Rush, Endacott & Rush stated in part: "It is understood by the parties herein that the services of Miss Adah Robinson have been secured and will be paid for by the owner. By reason of her contract, the church and the architects are to have benefit of her services. The architects agree to cooperate with her in all matters pertaining to the artistic features of the project."
   A second contract of the same date in the form of a letter from C. C. Cole to Adah Robinson delineated her official role: "... we desire your services, especially pertaining to all matters artistic, both in interior finish and outside design, you to cooperate with the architects and represent us in all matters of this nature."
23. For a comprehensive study and a list of resource material, see DeLong, pps. 61-66.
24. DeLong, p. 66.
25. Boston Avenue Methodist Episcopal Church, South, *A Twentieth Century Church* (Tulsa: Mid-West Printing Co., 1929), p. 31.
26. For five years preceeding World War I, Robert Garrison was first assistant to Gutzon Boruim. Later, in a worldwide competition he won the commission to do the sculpture on the Riverside Baptist Church in New York City.
27. Alfonso Iannelli, "The Boston Avenue Methodist Episcopal Church of Tulsa, Oklahoma," *Western Architect,* Vol. 38, October 1929, p. 190.
28. Sheldon Cheney, *New World Architecture* (London, New York, and Toronto: Longmans, Green and Co., 1930), p. 341.
29. Jenkin Lloyd Jones, "A House For A Cousin: The Richard Lloyd Jones House," *Frank Lloyd Wright Newsletter,* Vol. 2, 4th Quarter, 1979, p. 1.
30. Raymond Jontomas Wahl, "An Analysis of Westhope, The Richard Lloyd Jones House by Frank Lloyd Wright," Master's Thesis, University of Tulsa 1967, p. 24.
31. Wahl, p. 11.
32. Jones, p. 2.
33. Wahl, p. 13.
34. Frank Lloyd Wright, *A Testament* (New York: Bramhall House, 1957), p. 29.
35. Wahl, p. 55.
36. Jones, p. 2.

PWA

1. Personal interview with Joseph R. Koberling, Jr., Architect, 8 November 1979.
2. Col. Frank G. Jonah, "Description of the Tulsa Union Depot Facility." Unpublished report of the Chief Engineer. (St. Louis: St. Louis-San Francisco Railway Co., n.d.), p. 1.
3. "Obituary of Leland I. Shumway," *Tulsa World,* 25 June 1969, Sec. B, p. 9, col. 2.
4. Personal interview with Frederick Vance Kershner, Architect, 17 October 1979.
5. John Sand also modeled the panels for Tulsa's Booker T. Washington High School.
6. "Tomorrow's High School," *Time,* 16 February 1942, pp. 53-54.
7. "Webster High School Dedication Set," *Tulsa Tribune,* 2 November 1938, Sec. A, p. 13, col. 5.

STREAMLINE

1. Martin Greif, *Depression Modern: The Thirties Style in America* (New York: Universe Books, 1975), p. 24.
2. William M. Bulkeley, "To Preserve or Not? That Is the Question For a Neo-Neon Age," *The Wall Street Journal,* 28 March 1980, Sec. 1, p. 1.
3. Norman Bel Geddes, *Horizons* (Boston: Little, Brown and Co., 1932), p. 1.
4. Bevis Hillier, *The World of Art Deco* (New York: E. P. Dutton and Co., 1971), p. 23.

BIBLIOGRAPHY

Many of the special resources cited in this bibliography have been reproduced and are available in the Special Collections Division of McFarlin Library at the University of Tulsa.

BOOKS AND PAMPHLETS

Arwas, Victor. *Art Deco.* New York: St. Martin's Press, 1976.

Automobile Manufacturers of America. *Automobile Facts and Figures.* 2nd ed. Detroit: A.M.A., 1945.

Baeder, John. *Diners.* New York: Harry Abrams, 1978.

Blakey, Ellen Sue; Boman, Robbie; Downing, Jim; Hall, Ina; Hamill, John; Ridgway, Peggi. *The Tulsa Spirit.* Tulsa: Continental Heritage Press, 1979.

Boston Avenue Methodist Episcopal Church, South. *A Twentieth Century Church.* Tulsa: Mid-West Printing Co., 1929.

Bradely, Charles B. *Design in the Industrial Arts.* Peoria, Ill.: Manual Arts Press, 1946.

Burleigh, Manford, and Adams, Charles M. *Modern Bus Terminals and Post Houses.* Ypsilanti: Michigan University Lithoprinters, 1941.

Bush, Donald J. *The Streamlined Decade.* New York: George Braziller, 1975.

Butler, William. *Tulsa 75: A History of Tulsa, Oklahoma.* Tulsa: The Metropolitan Chamber of Commerce, 1974.

Cheney, Sheldon. *New World Architecture.* New York: Longmans, Green and Co., 1930.

Cheney, Sheldon and Martha. *Art and the Machine: An Account of Industrial Design in 20th Century America.* New York: McGraw-Hill Book Co., 1936.

Chicago Northwestern Terra Cotta Co. Catalogue. Chicago: 1938.

Christ the King Catholic Church. *Christ the King Church Golden Jubilee 1928-1978.* Tulsa: The Church, 1978.

Darling, Sharon S. *Chicago Ceramics & Glass: An Illustrated History from 1871 to 1933.* Chicago: Chicago Historical Society, 1979.

Debo, Angie. *Tulsa: From Creek Town to Oil Capital.* Norman: University of Oklahoma Press, 1943.

DeLong, David Gilson. *The Architecture of Bruce Goff.* New York: Garland Publishing, Inc., 1977.

Douglas, Clarence B. *The History of Tulsa: A City with a Personality.* Chicago/Tulsa: S. J. Clark Publishing Co., 1921.

Duis, Perry. *Chicago: Creating New Traditions.* Chicago: Chicago Historical Society, 1976.

Dunn, Nina Lane. *Tulsa's Magic Roots.* (n.p.): Oklahoma Book Publishing Co., 1979.

Ferriss, Hugh. *The Metropolis of Tomorrow.* New York: Washburn, 1929.

Frankl, Paul T. *New Dimensions.* New York: Payson and Clarke, 1928.
— *Form and Reform.* New York: Harper, 1930.

Galbreath, Frank. *Glenn Pool: And a Little Oil Town of Yesterday.* Privately printed in U.S.A. by Frank Galbreath, 1978.

Gebhard, David and Von Breton, Harriette. *Kem Weber: The Moderne in Southern California, 1920 through 1941.* University of California-Santa Barbara, 1976.
— *L. A. in the Thirties 1931-1941.* Los Angeles: Peregrine Smith, Inc. 1975.
— *The Richfield Building, 1928-1968.* New York: Atlantic Richfield Co., 1968.

Geddes, Norman Bel. *Horizons.* Boston: Little, Brown and Co., 1932.
— *Magic Motorways.* New York: Random House, 1940.

Geer, Walter. *The Story of Terra Cotta.* New York: Tobias A. Wright, 1920.

Greif, Martin. *Depression Modern: The Thirties Style in America.* New York: Universe Books, 1975.

Harris, Cyril M. *Dictionary of Architecture and Construction.* New York: McGraw-Hill, 1975.

Heyer, Paul, *Architects on Architecture: New Directions in America.* New York: Walker Publishing Co., 1978.

Hicks, John D. and Mowry, George E. *A Short History of American Democracy.* 2nd ed. Boston: Houghton-Mifflin, 1956.

Hillier, Bevis. *Art Deco.* London: Studio Vista Books, 1968.
— *Art Deco.* Minneapolis: Minneapolis Institute of Arts, 1971.
— *The World of Art Deco.* New York: E. P. Dutton and Co., 1971.

Hirshon, Paul and Izenour, Steve. *White Towers.* Cambridge: MIT Press, 1979.

Hitchcock, Henry-Russell. *In the Nature of Materials: The Buildings of Frank Lloyd Wright, 1887-1941.* New York: Da Capo Press, 1973.

Hoff, John David, Jr. "A History of Tulsa International Airport." Master's thesis. The University of Tulsa, 1967.

Hornbostel, Cleb. *Construction Materials: Types, Uses, and Applications.* New York: John Wiley & Sons, 1978
— *Materials for Architecture.* New York: Reinhold Publishing Corp., 1961.

Jordy, William H. *American Buildings and Their Architects.* New York: Doubleday, Anchor Books, 1972.
— *American Buildings and Their Architects: The Impact of European Modernism in the Mid-Twentieth Century.* New York: Doubleday, Anchor Books, 1976.

Laurence, Frederick S. *Color in Architecture.* New York: National Terra Cotta Society, 1924.

Leonard, R. L., and Glassgold, C. A. *Modern American Design.* New York: Washburn, 1930.

Mackertertich, Tony and Peter. *Facade.* London: M. M. Dunbar, 1976.

McMillian, Elizabeth. *Bullocks Wilshire, 1929-1979: A Legend Still.* Los Angeles: Bullocks Wilshire, 1979.

Meikle, Jeffrey L. *Twentieth Century Limited: Industrial Design in America, 1925-1939.* Philadelphia: Temple University, 1979.

Menten, Theodore. *The Art Deco Style: In Household Objects, Architecture, Sculpture, Graphics, Jewelry.* New York: Dover Publications, 1972.

Morris, Lerona Rosamond. *Tulsa — The City Beautiful.* [Tulsa?: n.p., 1927?]
— *Oklahoma Yesterday, Today and Tomorrow.* Guthrie, Ok.: Cooperative Publishing Co., 1930.

National Terra Cotta Society. *Terra Cotta of the Italian Renaissance.* New York: National Terra Cotta Society, 1925.

Polk's Tulsa City Directory. Kansas City: R. L. Polk, 1925-1942.

Roberts, Jennifer Davis. *Norman Bel Geddes.* Austin, Texas: University of Texas, 1979.

Robinson, Cervin, and Bletter, Rosemarie Haag. *Skyscraper Style: Art Deco New York.* New York: Oxford University Press, 1975.

Robinson, Karalyn, et al. *Portfolio: Art Deco Historic District, Miami Beach.* Miami Beach: Bucolo Preservation Press, 1979.

Ruskin, John. *The Works of John Ruskin: The Seven Lamps of Architecture.* New York: Crowell, nd.

Saylor, Henry H. *Dictionary of Architecture.* New York: John Wiley and Sons, Inc., 1963.

Scully, Vincent, Jr. *Masters of World Architecture: Frank Lloyd Wright.* New York: George Braziller, Inc., 1960.
— *Modern Architecture.* New York: George Braziller, Inc., 1965.

Semback, Klaus-Jurgen. *Into the Thirites Style and Design 1927-1934.* London: Thomas and Hudson, 1971.

Smith, R. C. *Materials of Construction.* New York: McGraw-Hill Book Co., 1979.

Teague, Walter Dorwin. *Design This Day: The Technique of Order in the Machine Age.* New York: Harcourt, Brace and Co., 1940.

Thoburn, Joseph B. and Wright, Muriel H. *History of Oklahoma.* New York: Lewis Historical Publishing Co., 1929.

U. S. Department of Transportation, Federal Highway Administration. *Highway Statistics, Summary to 1975.* Washington: GPO, 1975.

Van Doren, Harold. *Industrial Design: A Practical Guide.* New York: McGraw-Hill Book Co., 1940.

Varian, Elayne H. *American Art Deco Architecture.* New York: Finch College Museum of Art, 1975.

Vieyra, Daniel I. *Fill 'er Up: An Architectural History of America's Gas Stations.* New York: Macmillan Publishing Co., Inc., 1979.

Vlack, Don. *Art Deco Architecture: Architecture in New York 1920-1940.* New York: Harper and Row, 1974.

Wahl, Raymond Jontomas. "An Analysis of 'Westhope', the Richard Lloyd Jones house by Frank Lloyd Wright." Master's thesis, University of Tulsa, 1967.

The Warrior. Vol. 30. Tulsa: Daniel Webster High School, 1976.

Weiss, Peg. *The Art Deco Environment.* Syracuse: Everson Museum of Art, 1976.

Wright, Frank Lloyd. *A Testament.* New York: Bramhall House, 1957.
— *An Autobiography.* New York: Duell, Sloan and Pearce, 1948.

ARTICLES

Cannon, P. J. "Real Club Home for Our Members." *Tulsa Spirit,* August 1928, pp. 8-10.

"Canopy Goes Modern." *National Petroleum News,* 19 June 1938, p. 58.

Darling, Ernest Franklin. "A Monument to Free Enterprise." *Tulsa Magazine,* February 1979, p. 53.

"Deco Rated." *Industrial Design,* 18 (1971): 8-9.

"Depression Hits Ultra Modern." *Architecture and Engineering,* 112 (1933): 82-85.

Diamond of Mid-Continent Petroleum Corporation. Tulsa, Mid-Continent Petroleum Corporation, 1927-1940.

Downing, Jim. "Legacy of a 'Studhorse Note'." *Tulsa Magazine,* "Aviation Anniversary Section," July 1978, pp. 1-48.

"Empire Builds Chandeliers that Match Beauty in Tulsa's Most Awe-Inspiring Buildings." *Tulsa Spirit,* August 1929, p. 5.

Greenslade, Rush. "Tulsa Club's New Home." *Tulsa Spirit,* August 1928, p. 7.

Holden, William. "New Home of the Chamber of Commerce." *Tulsa Spirit,* August 1928, pp. 3-6.

Iannelli, Alfonso. "The Boston Avenue Methodist Church of Tulsa, Oklahoma." *Western Architect,* 38 (October 1929): 173-174.

Jones, Jenkin Lloyd. "A House for a Cousin, the Richard Lloyd Jones House." *Frank Lloyd Wright Newsletter,* 2 (4th quarter 1979): 1-3.

Kostka, Robert. "Bruce Goff and the New Tradition." *The Prairie School Review,* (2nd Quarter 1970): 5-15.

"KVOO, The Voice of Oklahoma." *Tulsa Spirit,* January 1928.

Lockhardt, William F. "Architectural Terra Cotta." *General Building Contractor,* January 1931, pp. 2-12.

"Marathon Builds Octagonal Station at Tulsa." *National Petroleum News,* 19 August 1931, p. 98.

Mooring, Stephen and Sergeant, John. "AD Profiles 16: Bruce Goff." *Architectural Design,* 48 (1978): 2-79.

"New Fronts for Old." *National Petroleum News,* 20 December 1933, p. 32-35.

"Oil Builds Good Towns to Live In." *National Petroleum News,* 5 February 1936, pp. 306-310.

"The Page Furniture Depository and Warehouse." *Art in Architecture,* 1 (1928): 11-13.

Payne, J. E. "Railroads Moving Forward." *Tulsa Spirit,* October 1935, p. 6.

Oppliger, William H. "Never Underestimate the Power of a Women." *Stained Glass,* 74 (Fall 1979): 219-222.

"Sand Springs Steps Forward." *Tulsa Spirit,* January 1930, p. 22.

Shaw, B. Russell. "A Model Airport Planned by Tulsa." *Southwest Air News,* October 1929, pp. 10, 20.

"Signs for Stations." *Petroleum Age,* September 1930, pp. 28-29

Spangle, R. S. "Twelve Floors? Furniture? in Tulsa at Genet's." *Tulsa Spirit,* March 1930, pp. 10-11.

"Standardized Service Stations Designed by Walter Dorwin Teague." *Architectural Record,* September 1937, pp. 69-72.

Texaco Star; for Employees of the Texas Company. Houston, Texas, 1925-1948.

This Week in Tulsa. 13 September 1930.

This Week in Tulsa. 9 May 1931.

"Tomorrow's High School." *Time Magazine,* 39 (February 1942): 53-54.

"1931 Trends in Station Design." *National Petroleum News,* 19 March 1930, pp. 105-136.

"Tulsa Arts Festival." *Tulsa World Magazine,* 11 February 1962.

"Tulsa Club is the Pride of Southwest." *Club Management,* February 1930.

"Tulsa Four State Fair." *Tulsa Spirit,* September 1935, pp. 5-6.

"Where Farmer and Merchant Meet." *Tulsa Spirit,* September 1931, p. 4.

White, L. R. "Oil Stations." *Architecture and Engineering,* 123 (1935): 28-36.

NEWSPAPERS

Brown, David. "Depot May Find New Station in Life." *Tulsa Daily World,* 29 February 1976.

Bulkeley, William M. "To preserve or not? That is the question for a Neo-Neon Age." *Wall Street Journal,* 28 March, 1980, pp. 1, 23.

"Chain Acquires Delman Movie." *Tulsa Tribune,* 15 March 1948, p. 11.

"Christ the King Praised in National Art Magazine." *Tulsa Daily World,* 3 March 1940.

"Crowds Throng Aisles as New Store is Opened." *Tulsa Daily World,* 3 December 1929, p. 1.

Curry, Virgil D. "Rails First Stirred Tulsa's Growth." *Tulsa Tribune,* 13 November 1932, p. 10.

"Day's Campaign Goal $400,000: Boston Methodist Church expects $50,000 from three persons." *Tulsa Daily World,* 8 December 1925, p. 1.

"Delman Opening Set for April 8." *Tulsa Daily World,* 28 March 1948, p. 6.

Dyer, John E. "Tulsa Depot was Showplace." *Tulsa Tribune,* 21 October 1970, p. 2B.

"Easy Listening, Radio Moves, Will Rogers Closing." *Tulsa Tribune.* 15 August 1977, p. 11.

"Endacott and Goff Designed New Grand Stand at Fairgrounds." *Tulsa Daily World,* Tulsa State Fair Section, 20 September 1931.

"Gala Opening Planned Tonight at Delman." *Tulsa Tribune,* 16 April 1948, p. 35.

Gideon, Russell. "And the Menu was Edged in Black." *Tulsa Daily World,* 20 January 1974, 'Your World Section' p. 3.

Hieronymus, Faith. "Doughnuts and the Tulsa Club." *Tulsa Daily World,* 1933.

Hieronymus, Faith. "Million Dollar Church Complete Modern Concept." *Tulsa Daily World,* Sunday Edition, 14 October 1928, p. 16.

"Modern Artistry for Medical Arts." *Tulsa Daily World,* 17 July 1927, p. 10.

"New Halliburton-Abbott Store Formally Open December 2." *Tulsa Daily World,* 24 November 1929, p. 1.

"New Lunch Room in Silver Castle." *Tulsa Daily World,* ? March 1936.

"Palace Theatre to be Made New." *Tulsa World,* 10 March 1935, p. 19.

Plummer, Martha. "From Cowpaths to Caps 'n' Gowns." *Tulsa Tribune,* 26 December 1955, p. 28.

"The 30's." *Tulsa Tribune,* "Midweek" 2 January 1980.

"Webster High School Dedication Set." *Tulsa Tribune,* 2 November 1938, p. 3.

Whitaker, Angie. "Christ the King Will Fete Monsignor." *Oklahoma Courier,* 6 February 1960.

HISTORICAL FILES

Boston Avenue United Methodist Church. (church archives) Tulsa, Ok.

Christ the King Catholic Church. (parish office files) Tulsa, Ok.

KVOO Radio. (company files) Station Office. Tulsa, Ok.

Northwestern Terra Cotta Company. (company files) Chicago, Ill.

Tulsa Central Library. (local history vertical files) Central Library. Reference Section. Tulsa, Ok.

The Tulsa Club. (history and photograph files) Club Office. Tulsa, Ok.

Tulsa County Historical Society. (local history files) Society Office, Tulsa City County Library, Central Library, Tulsa, Ok.

Tulsa International Airport. (airport history files) Office of Airport Administration. Tulsa, Ok.

The University of Tulsa. (local history vertical files) McFarlin Library. Tulsa, Ok.

ARCHITECTURAL PLANS

Noftsger, Gaylord, Architect, Oklahoma City. *Warehouse Market:* Office of McNulty Properties, Tulsa, Ok.

Smith & Senter, Architects, Tulsa. *Philcade:* Office of Dennis Manasco, Architect, Tulsa, Ok.

— *Tulsa Municipal Airport Terminal:* Office of Dennis Manasco, Architect, Tulsa, Ok.

St. Louis-San Francisco Railway Company (Frisco), *Tulsa Union Depot:* Office of the Architect, St. Louis, Mo.

EPHEMERAL SOURCES

Atkinson, A. M. Unpublished notes on Christ the King Church, ca. 1930. Parish Office scrapbook. Collection Christ the King Catholic Church, Tulsa, Ok.

Bartholomew, Harland. Unpublished preliminary report on a Civic Center. Harland Bartholomew and Associates, St. Louis, Missouri, 21 May 1930. Collection Tulsa County Historical Society.

Byrne, Barry. Unpublished notes for Father Fletcher on Christ the King Church, December, 1939. Parish Office scrapbook. Collection Christ the King Catholic Church, Tulsa, Ok.

— "Why Teach Art in Church." (TS speech) National Convention of the Catholic Art Association. Tulsa, Ok. 28 November 1974. Collection Christ the King Catholic Church, Tulsa, OK.

Koberling, Joseph R., Jr. "Reminiscences." (TS speech) Will Rogers High School Assembly. Tulsa, Ok. 6 November 1979. Private collection.

Saunders, Edward W. Unpublished manuscript diary of the architect, ca. 1930. Private collection.

Senter, Leon B. Unpublished scrapbooks of the architect, ca. 1920-1960. Private collection.

Schillinger, Cindy. *Boston Avenue Church: Heritage and Destiny,* 1978. (TS media presentation) Collection Boston Avenue Methodist Church, Tulsa, Ok.

Unpublished history of Marquette School, nd. Collection Christ the King Catholic Church, Tulsa, Ok.

Unpublished notes on the church interior, nd. Collection Christ the King Catholic Church, Tulsa, Ok.

Unpublished notes on the development of Christ the King Parish, nd. Collection Christ the King Catholic Church, Tulsa, Ok.

Will Rogers Theatre. Opening night program, 21 July 1941. Private collection.

INTERVIEWS

Arnot, Imogene. Personal. 11 October 1979.

Ball, Ben. Telephone. 23 January 1980.

Bendel, Mrs. Ralph. Telephone. October 1979, January 1980.

Bliss, Mrs. Charles W. Telephone. November, December 1979.

Bliss, John. Telephone. November, December 1979.

Blue, Harry B. Telephone. April 1980.

Bragdon, Earl. Personal. 23 January 1980.

Brooks, Rev. Donald W. Telephone. 26 November 1979.

Burns, K. C. Telephone. January 1980.

Choate, Louise. Personal. 25 November 1979.

Clinton, Walton. Personal. February 1980. Telephone. January 1980.

Cole, Mary Caroline. Personal. 5 November 1979.

De Vinna, Maurice. Personal. 30 November 1979.

Duncan, J. C. Telephone. January 1980.

Elsner, John. Telephone. October 1979.

Farmer, Mrs. A. L. Personal. 4 January, 15 March 1980.

Gideon, Russell. Personal. 13 November 1979.

Goff, Bruce. Personal. 11 October 1979, 6 February 1980.

Holmes, Dan P. Personal. 7 March 1980.

Holliman, Maxine. Personal. 19 October 1979.

Hrdy, Olinka. Personal. 11 April 1980.

Jones, Mrs. Donald. Telephone. October 1979.

Jordan, Ray. Telephone. 12 November 1979.

Kershner, Frederick Vance. Personal. 17 October 1979, January 1980. Telephone. 18 October 1979.

Koberling, Joseph R., Jr. Personal. 21 September, 6 November, 8 November, 20 November 1979, 27 February 1980. Telephone. January 1980.

Kristiansen, Trygve. Personal. December 1979, January 1980.

KVOO Radio Staff. Personal. 7 January 1980.

LaTroph, Alan. Telephone. December 1979.

Lieberman, Jim. Personal. 9 January 1980.

McCollum, Mrs. J. W. Telephone. 10 January 1980.

McCormick, Donald. Telephone. 12 December 1979.

Meeks, Sharon. Personal. 6 November 1979.

Monnet, Annabelle. Personal. 5 October 1979.

Murphy, Paul. Telephone. January 1980.

Page, Scottie. Telephone. 1 November 1979.

Parkey, I. H. Personal. January, February, March 1980. Telephone. January, February, March 1980.

Pickard, Dr. Rick. Personal. November 1979.

Primm, H. P. Personal. 28 March 1980.

Reen, A. J. Telephone. December 1979.
Schupert, Jack. Telephone. January 1980.
Shumway, Mrs. L. I. Telephone.
    October 1979.
Stewart, Jon. Personal. 7 January 1980.
Ungerman, Mrs. Arnold. Telephone.
    28 November 1979.
Walker, Clyde. Telephone. January 1980.
Waller, William. Telephone.
    December 1979.
West, Robert. Personal. 8 November 1979.
    Telephone. 28 November 1979.
Whitacre, Jack. Telephone.
    23 January 1980.
White, Rev. James D. Telephone.
    26 November 1979.
Whitlock, Mrs. A. S. Personal.
    8 January 1980.
Wieman, Ernest. Personal. 27 March 1980.
Wiesendanger, Martin. Personal. Fall 1979.
Wixson, Douglas. Telephone.
    January 1980.

ARCHITECTURAL PROFESSION INTERVIEWS

*Numbers following citations correspond
to those in the Architectural Profession
Section of this book and indicate subject
of the interview.*

Abshire, Mrs. Carl. Daughter of
    A. T. Thorne. Telephone. November
    1979, (38, 42).
Barnard, H. G. Personal.
    8 October 1979, (15).
Baze, Ross B. Telephone. December 1979,
    January 1980. (2, 32).
Black, Mrs. Ralph. Telephone.
    November 1979. (4).
Black, Ralph M. Jr. Telephone.
    November 1979. (4).
Blair, Mrs. John T. Telephone.
    October 1979. (5).
Blue, Clarence H. Son of Lawrence E. Blue.
    Telephone. 16 December 1979. (6, 21).
Bragdon, Earl. Personal. 26 October 1979.
    (14, 16, 19, 20, 22, 24, 29, 31, 37,
    38, 39, 45, 47, 48).
Broach, David. Personal. April 1980. (19).
Bryant, Dr. John. School of Architecture,
    Oklahoma State University.
    Telephone. January 1980. (33).
Calderwood, Mrs. William Henry Cameron.
    Telephone. December 1979. (8).
Calderwood, Nancy. Daughter-in-law.
    Telephone. October 1979. (8).
Chamberlaine, Dr. George. School of
    Architecture, Oklahoma State University.
    Telephone. January 1980. (33).
Clary, Virginia B. Daughter of John Blair.
    Telephone. October 1979. (5).
Clinton, Walton. Telephone. February,
    April 1980. (35, 41, 44).
Cross, Marshall Canfield, Jr. Telephone.
    November 1979. (9).
DeLong, Dr. David. Telephone.
    December 1979. (17).
Duggan, Mrs. Frederick Alexander.
    Telephone. October 1979. (9, 11, 29).

Eaton, Dr. Leonard. Architectural
    Historian, University of Michigan.
    Telephone. November 1979. (36).
Endacott, Jack A. Son of Asbury Endacott.
    Telephone. November 1979. (12).
Endacott, Mark. Son of Asbury Endacott.
    Telephone. November 1979. (12).
Endacott, Richard. Nephew of Asbury
    Endacott. November 1979. (12).
Forsyth, Mrs. Edith Deal Ache. Telephone.
    October 1979, November 1979. (15).
Gillian, Justine. Secretary to
    A. M. Atkinson. Personal.
    March 1980. (1).
Goff, Bruce. Personal. 11 October 1979.
    Telephone. November 1979.
    (7, 12, 17, 36).
Hamm, Mrs. Earl N. Daughter of William
    Alva Fry. Telephone.
    November 1979. (16).
Huckett, Richard. Telephone.
    December 1979. (23).
Kershner, Frederick Vance. Personal.
    17 October, December 1979.
    Telephone. December 1979.
    (1, 13, 15, 20, 25, 30, 38, 39).
Knoblock, Mrs. C. C. Sister-in-law of
    Fred Knoblock. Telephone.
    November, December 1979. (21).
Koberling, Joseph R., Jr. Personal.
    21 September, 2 November, December
    1979. Telephone. January 1980.
    (1, 4, 12, 14, 17, 19, 21, 24, 27, 29,
    31, 33, 35, 39, 45).
Kubatzky, Theodore. Grandson of
    Otto Kubatzky. Telephone.
    November 1979. (23).
Manasco, Dennis. Last partner of Leon
    Senter. Personal. March 1980. (38).
Marrs, Mrs. A. Garland. Daughter of
    Lymann Howland Ruggles. Telephone.
    December 1979. (35).
McCormick, Donald. Personal. 30 October
    1979. Telephone. November 1979,
    January 1980. (4, 15, 25, 38, 45).
McCormick, Mrs. Donald. Sister of Ross
    Baze. Telephone. February 1980. (2).
McCune, Gordon. Son of Malcolm
    McCune. Telephone.
    February 1980. (26).
McCune, Mrs. Malcolm. Telephone.
    February 1980. (26).
Murphy, John T. Last partner Keene &
    Simpson. Telephone.
    December 1979. (18, 40).
Murray, David G. Last partner of
    A. M. Atkinson. Telephone.
    November 1979. (1).
Nelson, Beverly, Jr. Telephone.
    November 1979. (28, 30).
Olsen, Gordon. Librarian, Kent County
    Library, Grand Rapids, Michigan.
    Telephone. December 1979. (36).
Olston, Mrs. Frank Michael. Telephone.
    February 1980. (1, 31).
Perry, Sequoyah. Turner Corporation.
    Telephone. April 1979. (44).
Perryman, Mrs. P. W. Daughter of Leon
    Senter. Telephone. November 1979.
    Personal. April 1980. (16, 38).

Pieffer, Bruce. Archivist, Frank Lloyd
    Wright Foundation. Telephone.
    April 1980. (48).
Price, Mrs. Harley T. Daughter of
    Frank Walter. Telephone.
    April 1980. (43).
Reid, John. Last partner of George Winkler.
    Telephone. March 1980. (46).
Saunders, Edward. Son of Edward
    Watkins Saunders. Telephone.
    October 1979. (37).
Shumway, J. F. Son of Leland Shumway.
    Telephone. November 1979. (39).
Sippel, Dr. Mary Edna. Wife of Erich
    Sippel. Telephone.
    November 1979. (41).
Thomas, Ken. Architectural Historian,
    City Hall, Atlanta, Ga. Telephone.
    March 1980. (43).
West, Robert Edward. Personal.
    8 November, December 1979.
    Telephone. January 1980.
    (4, 15, 19, 28, 45).
Wilber, Mrs. Phillip H. Telephone.
    January 1980. (33).
Wilson, Mrs. Edward. Daughter of Harry
    Mahler. Telephone. October 1979,
    February 1980. (29).
Winkler, George, Jr. Telephone.
    March 1980. (46).
Winter, Mrs. H. M. Granddaughter of
    Frank Walter. Telephone.
    March 1980. (43).
Wolaver, William. Telephone. November,
    December 1979, January 1980.
    (1, 6, 15, 19, 38, 39, 47).
Wozencraft, Wallace O. Telephone.
    March 1980. (4, 45).

ILLUSTRATION SOURCES

Courtesy Mrs. Howard G. Barnett, Tulsa, Oklahoma: 91.
Courtesy Beryl D. Ford Collection, Tulsa, Oklahoma: 35, 38, 102, 115, 157.
Courtesy Bruce Goff Collection, Tyler, Texas: 74, 76 (left), 77, 78, 79, 83, 90.
Photographs by David Halpern, Tulsa, Oklahoma: cover, 36, 39, 41, 42, 45, 51, 52, 54, 55, 57, 59, 60, 62, 65, 66, 67, 69, 70, 72, 73 (right), 84,
    85, 86, 87, 88, 89, 92, 93, 106, 107, 109, 110, 111, 112, 120, 121, 122, 123, 124, 125, 126, 127, 129, 130, 131, 132, 145, 148, 150 (left), 151,
    153, 154, 160, 161, 162, 163, 164, 165, 166, 167, 168, 169, 170, 171, 172, 173, 174, 175, 176, 177, 178.
Photographs by Howard Hopkins, Tulsa, Oklahoma: 48 (right), 155 (right).
Courtesy Olinka Hrdy, Praque, Oklahoma: 80.
Courtesy Dennis Manasco, Tulsa, Oklahoma: 50, 56, 116, 117.
Photographs by Bob McCormack, Tulsa, Oklahoma: 76 (right), 108.
Courtesy Donald McCormick, Architect, Tulsa, Oklahoma: 141.
Courtesy Mrs. Murray McCune, Tulsa, Oklahoma: 94.
Courtesy McNulty Properties, Tulsa, Oklahoma: 61.
Courtesy Metropolitan Tulsa Chamber of Commerce: 44, 48 (left), 101, 119.
National Petroleum News, August, 1931: 142.
National Petroleum News, June, 1938: 143.
Newspaper Printing Corporation, Tulsa, Oklahoma: 155 (left).
Courtesy I. H. Parkey, Tulsa, Oklahoma: 146, 147.
Petroleum Age, January, 1934: 140.
Courtesy Public Service Company of Oklahoma, Tulsa, Oklahoma: 37.
Courtesy St. Louis-San Francisco Railway Company, St. Louis, Missouri: 101, 103, 104, 105.
Courtesy Mrs. Jack Talbot, Tulsa, Oklahoma: 33.
Courtesy Tulsa Board of Adjustments: 63.
Courtesy Tulsa Club Archives: 73 (left).
Courtesy Tulsa Historic Preservation Office: 43.
Courtesy Tulsa International Airport Archives: 114.
Courtesy Mrs. A. S. Whitlock, Tulsa, Oklahoma: 150 (right).

INDEX

terra cotta, 31-32, 109, 114, 125, 128
    French influence on, 57
    polychromed, examples of, 61, 108-109
    sculpture, 82
"Terra Cotta City," 32
Texaco, 144
    service station, 22, 25, 144; *145*
Texas Oil Company, *see* Texaco
Thompson, Noble, 53
Thorne, Alexander Thompson, 191
Transok Building, *see* Public Service
    Company of Oklahoma
Tulsa,
    metropolitan development, 22-23
    population of, 64
Tulsa Building, *see* Tulsa Club
Tulsa Airport Corporation, 118
Tulsa Building Corporation, 73
Tulsa Club, 25, 73-75, 91; *73-74*
    addition to, 75
Tulsa Chamber of Commerce, 73
Tulsa Fire Alarm Building, 24, 109,
    113; *109-112*
Tulsa Iron and Wire Works, 47
Tulsa Monument Company, 150, 152; *153*
    glass sandblasting, 46
Tulsa Municipal Airport Administration
    Building, 24, 99, 113-114, 118;
    115-117
    proposed building, 24, 114, *114*
Tulsa Ornamental Iron Company, 47
Tulsa State Fairground Pavilion, 24, 108;
    106-108
Tulsa Union Depot, 24, 47, 58, 99, 100,
    104-105; *101-105*
Type Service Corporation, *see* Midwest
    Marble and Tile
Tyrrell, Harry C., 42, 46

U

Ungerman, Dr. Arnold, 165
Ungerman (Arnold) residence, 165;
    164-165
Union Bus Depot, 24, 118-120; *119-121*
Union Depot, *see* Tulsa Union Depot
United States Post Office, 58, 99

V

vitrolite, 137, 143
    decorative use of, 143, 149
"Voice of Oklahoma," *see* KVOO Radio

W

Wagner, Otto, 24
Walker, W. Frank, 53
Walter, Frank C., 23, 40, 191; *38-39,*
    41-42
Walters, Clarence Dillworth, 191
Warehouse Market, 23, 59-61; *60-61*
Weary and Alford, 23
Weber, Kem, 137
Webster (Daniel) High School, 24, 122,
    128-132; *129-132*
West, L. G., 152
West, Robert E., 25, 191-192
Westhope, 25, 91-95; *91-94*
Whenthoff, William D., 170
Whenthoff (William D.) residence,
    170; *172*

Whitlock, A. S., 150
Whitlock's Grocery Store, 150; *150*
Whittier Square, 149
Will Rogers High School, *see* Rogers
    (Will) High School
Will Rogers Theater, 25, 154-155; *156*
windows, 78
    corner & ribbon, 137
    stained glass, 68-69
Winkler, George, 192
Wixson, Douglas, 143
Wolaver, William H., 24, 130, 161, 192;
    129-132, 162-163
Wonderland Theater, *see* Palace Theater
Works Progress Administration (WPA),
    100, 120, 122, *see also* Public Works
    Administration (PWA)
World War II,
    effect on building, 31
Wright, Frank Lloyd, 20, 22, 24-25,
    64-65, 78, 81, 91, 192; *91-94*
    Usonion period, 95
Wright, John Lloyd, 68
Wright, Lloyd, 20, 24

Z

Zigzag style, 18, 31
    design elements of, 19, 31
    popular response to, 63

This book was designed by Phillips Knight Walsh, Inc.
Typography is Alphatype Garamond set by Type 1, Inc.
Color separations were done by United Graphics, Inc.
Text paper is Warren Lustro Offset Enamel from Tulsa Paper Company.
Printing was done on Miller and Planeta presses by R. F. Rodgers Lithographing Company.
Bookbinding was done by Nicholstone Book Bindery, Inc. in Nashville, Tennessee.